Lets Hack The Tech

Shashwat Jain

Shashwat Jain

Shashwat Jain asserts the moral rights to be identified as the author of this work.

This book is designed to provide accurate and authoritative information for the students interested in Cyber Security/ Ethical Hacking. It is sold under the express understanding that any decisions or actions you take as a result of reading this book must be based on your judgment and will be at your sole risk. The author will not be held responsible for the consequences of any action/s and/or decisions taken as a result of any information given or recommendations made.

ACKNOWLEDGMENT

Many thanks to all whose support, care and motivation helped me and spurred me on in the writing of this book I am especially grateful to my family for their encouragement and thoughtful words that always came at the right time, providing the needed drive to make this book a success. For the valuable help they rendered throughout this project, I really do appreciate. Their support and love kept me going - ensuring I never entertained the thought of relenting until my aim was achieved. They are the best partners I can ever dream of and they given me their absolute best!

TABLE OF CONTENTS

INTRODUCTION

Everyone who works on an electronic device mus be familiar with the term "Cyber Crime." Initially, when a man invented computer or mobile and then the technology for communicating between them was evolved, he would have never thought that the cyber space he is creating could be flooded with any sort of crime i.e. cyber crime. But now almost all of us might have heard the term cyber crime, e-crime, hi-tech crime which is nothing but an activity that involves a computer and a network. The computer may have been used in the commission of a crime, or it may be the target. Cybercrime may harm someone's security and financial health. To say in one line, "Cyber crime refers to all the activities done with criminal intent in cyberspace."

What is Cyber Crime?

- ✔ Cybercrime or a computer crime is any crime that involves a computer and a network.
- ✔ The computer used in the commission of a crime or may be the target.
- ✔ Both governmental and non-state actors engage in cybercrimes.
- ✔ Annual damage to global economy is about $445 Billion.

You may be wondering why one should know about Cyber crime?

Most of us are using internet and mobiles as per data 41% of India's population i.e. about 55cr. people use internet and in that also about 40-45% people use it for online transactions. So if your personal information goes in wrong hands you can become bankrupt.

How to identify if I'm a previous victim of cyber crime or not?

If you start receiving absurd mails or your email account gets flooded with unwanted mails; means you have become a victim of Cyber crime.

The hacker's main aim is to disrupt a system or network. Whether he is a White, Grey or a Black hat hacker his level of destruction is to stop or get the access to the computer systems. Repeated hacking or tampering constantly might take a hacker behind bars but many times these crimes are taken lightly.

Some more Stats

According to NCRB, India reported 50,035 cyber crimes in 2020; 44,546 cases in 2019 and 27,248 cases in 2018. The year 2020 saw 4,047 cases of online banking fraud; 2,160 cases of ATM fraud; 1,194 credit/debit card fraud and 1,093 OTP frauds. Reports of 2021-22 are still awaited.

What is hacking?

A commonly used hacking definition is the act of compromising digital devices and networks through unauthorized access to an account or computer system. Hacking is not always a malicious act, but it is most commonly associated with illegal activity and data theft by cyber criminals.

Hacking refers to the misuse of devices like computers, smartphones, tablets, and networks to cause damage to or corrupt systems, gather information on users, steal data and documents, or disrupt data-related activity.

A traditional view of hackers is a lone rogue programmer who is highly skilled in coding and modifying computer software and hardware systems. But this narrow view does not cover the true technical nature of hacking. Hackers are increasingly growing in sophistication, using stealthy attack methods designed to go completely unnoticed by Cybersecurity software and IT teams. They are also highly skilled in creating attack vectors that trick users into opening malicious attachments or links and freely giving up their sensitive personal data.

As a result, modern-day hacking involves far more than just an angry kid in their bedroom. It is a multi-billion-dollar industry with extremely sophisticated and successful techniques.

History of Hacking/Hackers

Hacking first appeared as a term in the 1970s but became more popular through the next decade. An article in a 1980 edition of Psychology Today ran the headline "The Hacker Papers" in an exploration of computer usage's addictive nature. Two years later, two movies, Tron and War Games, were released, in which the lead characters set about hacking into computer systems, which introduced the concept of hacking to a wide audience and as a potential national security risk. Sure enough, later that year, a group of teenagers cracked the computer systems of major organizations like Los Alamos National Laboratory, Security Pacific Bank, and Sloan-Kettering Cancer Center. A Newsweek article covering the event became the first to use the word "hacker" in the negative light it now holds.

This event also led Congress to pass several bills around computer crimes, but that did not stop the number of high-profile attacks on corporate and government systems. Of course, the concept of hacking has spiraled with the release of the public internet, which has led to far more opportunities and more lucrative rewards for hacking activity. This saw techniques evolve and increase in sophistication and gave birth to a wide range of types of hacking and hackers.

Types of Hacking/Hackers

There are typically four key drivers that lead to bad actors hacking websites or systems: (1) financial gain through the theft of credit card details or by defrauding financial services, (2) corporate espionage, (3) to gain notoriety or respect for their hacking talents, and (4) state-sponsored hacking that aims to steal business information and national intelligence. On top of that, there are politically motivated hackers who aim to raise public attention by leaking sensitive information, such as Anonymous, LulzSec, and WikiLeaks.

A few of the most common types of hackers that carry out these activities involve:

Black Hat Hackers

Black hat hackers are the "bad guys" of the hacking scene. They go out of their way to discover vulnerabilities in computer systems and software to exploit them for financial gain or for more malicious purposes, such as to gain reputation, carry out corporate espionage, or as part of a nation-state hacking campaign. These individuals' actions can inflict serious damage on both computer users and the organizations they work for. They can steal sensitive personal information, compromise computer and financial systems, and alter or take down the functionality of websites and critical networks.

White Hat Hackers

White hat hackers can be seen as the "good guys" who attempt to prevent the success of black hat hackers through proactive hacking. They use their technical skills to break into systems to assess and test the level of network security, also known as ethical hacking. This helps expose vulnerabilities in systems before black hat hackers can detect and exploit them. The techniques white hat hackers use are similar to or even identical to those of black hat hackers, but these individuals are hired by organizations to test and discover potential holes in their security defenses.

Grey Hat Hackers

Grey hat hackers sit somewhere between the good and the bad guys. Unlike black hat hackers, they attempt to violate standards and principles but without intending to do harm or gain financially. Their actions are typically carried out for the common good. For example, they may exploit a vulnerability to raise awareness that it exists, but unlike white hat hackers, they do so publicly. This alerts malicious actors to the existence of the vulnerability.

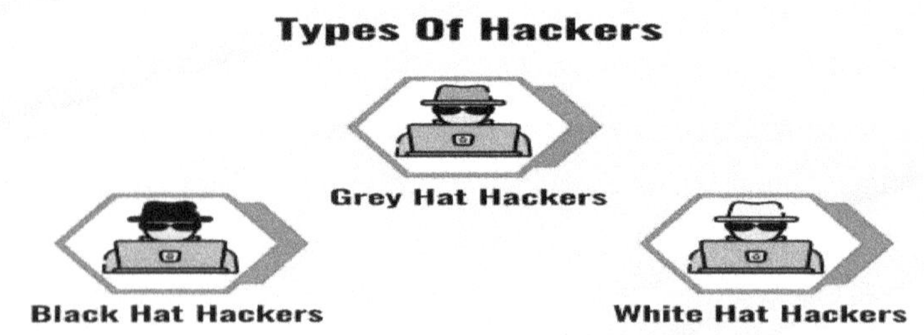

Devices Most Vulnerable To Hacking

Smart Devices

Smart devices, such as smartphones, are lucrative targets for hackers. Android devices, in particular, have a more open-source and inconsistent software development process than Apple devices, which puts them at risk of data theft or corruption. However, hackers are increasingly targeting the millions of devices connected to the Internet of Things (IoT).

Webcams

Webcams built into computers are a common hacking target, mainly because hacking them is a simple process. Hackers typically gain access to a computer using a Remote Access Trojan (RAT) in rootkit malware, which allows them to not only spy on users but also read their messages, see their browsing activity, take screenshots, and hijack their webcam.

Routers

Hacking routers enables an attacker to gain access to data sent and received across them and networks that are accessed on them. Hackers can also hijack a router to carry out wider malicious acts such as distributed denial-of-service (DDoS) attacks, Domain Name System (DNS) spoofing, or cryptomining.

Email

Email is one of the most common targets of cyberattacks. It is used to spread malware and ransomware and as a tactic for phishing attacks, which enable attackers to target victims with malicious attachments or links.

Jailbroken Phones

Jailbreaking a phone means removing restrictions imposed on its operating system to enable the user to install applications or other software not available through its official app store. Aside from being a violation of the end-user's license agreement with the phone developer, jailbreaking exposes many vulnerabilities. Hackers can target jailbroken phones, which allows them to steal any data on the device but also extend their attack to connected networks and systems.

Traditional Cyber Crimes

Criminals whose focus is on monetary gains only are called traditional cyber criminals. Most of them are identified as some internal source. Recent study has confirmed that almost 80% offenders of such crimes belong to the related company or firm. Industrial espionage, intellectual property crime, trademark violation, illegal fund transfers, credit card scams, etc. are some of the traditional cyber crimes. Such criminals who conduct these crimes are more likely to end up behind bars if the crime is proved.

Cyber Threats:

Stolen data are circulated as against the intellectual property laws according to such ideology threats. These criminals consider themselves as Robin Hood and spread the data which is preserved under intellectual property rights. Many terrorist activities are also termed as ideology threats in the cyber world. They spread their own ideology or oppose government's by using the internet technology. Cyberanarchistsis how they are called and their primary aim is to cover their ideology or principles and opposing what is against their activities. Many terrorists' plans and data's are also considered as cyber threats.Thus whatever be the nature of cyber crime strict laws must be administered to enable a secured cyber space. As more and more of our daily activities becomes connected or interlinked in cyber space the need for a complete secure technology has become the need of the hour. Whether it is simple email hacking or phishing, the people involved in such activities are definitely invading the privacy of individuals and business organizations. Identity thefts, money swindling, and credit card scams are grave issues which can cause irreparable damage to the person concerned.

ESSENTIALS FOR A HACKER

Step 1: **Learn To Program In C**

C programming being one of the most powerful languages in computer programming, It is necessary to really master this language. This programming language was invented Denise Ritchie in between the years 1969 and 1973 at AT&T by Bell Labs. C programming will essentially help you divide the task in smaller pieces and these pieces can be expressed by a sequence of commands. Try writing some program on your own by assessing the logic.

Step 2: **Learn More Than One Programming Language**

When you are trying to become a hacker, it is very important to learn other modern computer programming languages such as JAVA, Perl, PHP and Python. One of the best ways to learn these is by reading books from experts. It will also help to know about markup languages like XML, HTML and data formats such as Json, Protobuf and others which are common way to transfer data between client and server.

Java is one of the most popular programming languages. It has been claimed that its also very secure. Knowing Java security model will empower you to understand how this language achieve security. Learn about the security loop holes in Java language and related frameworks. Pick and read from many free PDF, tutorials and ebooks available to learn java online.

Perl is a general purpose dynamic programming language, which is high level and can be interpreted. This language borrows some features of C language. On the other hand, JAVA is concurrent, class based and objects oriented programming language. Python is really handy when you are trying to automate some repetitive tasks.

HTML is the mark up language based on which the web pages are designed, created and displayed. The web browsers read the HTML code to display the web page.

Python is best language for web development and favorite language of an lot of programmer due to its simplicity and quick turn around. A lot of people use Python to do simple and complex automation.

Step 3: **Learn UNIX**

UNIX is a multi-tasking and multi-user computer operating system that is designed to provide good security to the systems. This operating system was developed by some employees of AT&T in Bell Labs.The best way to learn it is to get into an open-source version [e.g. centos) and install/run the same on your own. You can operate internet without learning UNIX, but it is not possible for you to be an internet hacker without understanding UNIX.

If you have not used Unix operating system yet, an few essential linux commands will make your comfortable in getting quickly started. A large number of web servers are hosted on Unix based servers and knowing internal of this operating system is going to be really a big boost in your skills.

Step 4: **Learn More Than one OS**

There are many other operating systems apart from UNIX, Windows operating system is one of the most commonly compromised systems, hence it is good to learn hacking Microsoft systems, which are closed-source systems.

According to the National Vulnerability Database, Microsoft operating systems have a large number of vulnerabilities.

Windows OS installers are distributed in binary, therefore it is not easy for you to read the code. Binary code is the digital representation of text and data that computer understands. However, knowing how programs are written for windows and how different applications behave on this operating system will help.

One of the recent vulnerabilities of a popular OS was that Java Web Start applications get launched automatically even if the Java plug-ins are disabled. Becoming a hacker is about knowing the weaknesses of these operating systems and targeting them systematically.

Step 5: **Learn Networking Concepts**

The networking concept needs to be sharp when you want to be a hacker.
Understanding how the networks are created is important, however you need to know the differences between different types of networks. Having a clear understanding of TCP/IP and UDP protocol is a must to be able to exploit the vulnerabilities on WWW.

Understand what is subnet, LAN, WAN and VPN.

The networking commands to do an HTTP request needs to be on your fingertips. The HTTP protocol, is the gateway through which one enters the internet world. Hence it is necessary to learn this protocol in order to break the barriers. The hackers often use the HTTP gateway to breach the security of the system and take control over it.

Apache Httpd is one of the most commonly used web servers and knowing in and out of it is going to empower you on any HTTP or other application layer protocol related endeavors.

Nmap is a powerful network scanning tool that is used by hackers and security professional across the world to identify vulnerable hosts. However, to effectively start using it you must understand the networking basics. To get advanced skills on NMap you can refer the book by creators -

Nmap Network Scanning: The Official Nmap Project Guide to Network Discovery and Security Scanning.

Step 6: Start Simple: Read Some Tutorials About Hacking

This is the simple and best way to start. Read as many tutorials as possible that are meant for hacking. These articles will give you insight and help you develop the attitude to be a hacker. Some tutorials will initiate you with Nmap, Nessus and SuperScan, some of the hacking programs or tools that hackers generally use. These tutorials a readily available over the internet; Both text and tutorials are available for you to answer your question how to be a hacker.

Step 7: **Learn Cryptography**

As an expert hacker, you need to understand and master the art of cryptography. The technology of cryptography and encryption is very important for internet and networkingh is the practice and study of techniques that are used for secure communication in the presence of the third parties. The encryption is done for various aspects of information security such as confidentiality of the data integrity of the data and authentication. Moreover, the technology of cryptography is extensively used in ATM cards, computer passwords and e-commerce. While hacking these encrypted codes needs to be broken, which is called decryption.

Cryptography is heavily used in SSL based internet communication. A expert hacker should be able to understand how SSL works and what is the importance of cryptography in keeping SSI. secure.

Understand various techniques used for password cracking. There are dozens of tools available to do password cracking and using it is not hacking.To be expert at hacking its important for you to understand how to create a program that can crack a password from cypher tool.

Step 8: **Experiment A Lot**

This is an important step for setting yourself up as an expert hacker. Setup a laboratory on your own to experiment the learning on the practical applications. A simplest lab will have your computer, however once you advance you may want to add more and more computers and required hardware for your experiments.

It is good to try experimenting on your own computers, where you can rectify if you have done any mistake.Many hackers initially start off by downloading virtual lab applications such as Oracle VirtualBox. You require at least 3 GBS of RAM and a comparatively powerful processor to carry out your hacking experiments. Setting up the virtual machine is crucial, as it will allow you to test virus, applications and different servers without affecting your own PC.

Some of the things you may need to keep in mind when doing experiments:-
- ➢ Keep a backup before any experiment.
- ➢ Start small and have check points.
- ➢ Know when to stop.
- ➢ Document your progress.
- ➢ Keep improvising.
- ➢ Automate repetitive tasks.

TYPES OF HACKING

Hacking is usually meant to break a code. There are three sections of hacking which are Web Hacking, Exploit Writing & Reverse Engineering and each of it requires different programming language.

1. Web Hacking

Since most of the tech is build around world wide web, it is important to learn web hacking to be a good hacker. Let's say you are interested in hacking web apps and/or websites then you will need to learn web coding. Websites use mostly HTML, PHP, and JavaScript so it is important to learn these three.

HTML:

One of the easiest and widely used static markup web language present in each and every website you see in your browser. It's recommended to learn HTML because it helps understanding web actions, response, and logic.

JavaScript:

JavaScript, often abbreviated JS, is a programming language that is one of the core technologies of the World Wide Web, alongside HTML and CSS. As of 2022, 98% of websites use JavaScript on the client side for webpage behavior, often incorporating third-party libraries. It helps to understand client-side mechanism which is essential for finding client-side flaws.

PHP:

PHP is a general-purpose scripting language geared toward web development. It was originally created by Danish-Canadian programmer Rasmus Lerdorf in 1994. The PHP reference implementation is now produced by The PHP Group.

SQL:

SQL is a domain-specific language used in programming and designed for managing data held in a relational database management system, or for stream processing in a relational data stream management system.

2. Exploit Writing

After web hacking, another most important feature of hacking is exploits. You can crack a particular software by writing an exploit. But to write an exploit you need to learn either Python or Ruby.

Python

It is said that a security researcher or a hacker should know Python because it is the core language for creating exploits and tools. Security experts and even pro hackers suggest that master python is the best way to learn hacking. Python offers wider flexibility and you can create exploits only if you are good in Python.

Ruby

Ruby is very simple yet complicated object-oriented language. Ruby is very useful when it comes to exploit writing. It is used for meterpreter scripting by hackers. The most famous hacker tool, Metasploit framework is programmed in Ruby. Though Ruby may not be versatile as Python, knowledge of Ruby is must in understanding exploits.

3. Reverse Engineering

Reverse engineering, the process of taking a software program's binary code and recreating it so as to trace it back to the original source code. If you know reverse engineering you can find flaws and bugs easily. If you want to learn reverse engineering you need to know C, C++ and Java. The process of converting the code written in high level language into an low level language without changing the original program is known as reverse engineering.

Phases of Hacking

Hacking is broken up into five phases: Reconnaissance, Scanning, Gaining Access, Maintaining Access, and finally Clearing tracks. The more you get close to all phases, the more stealth will be your your attack.

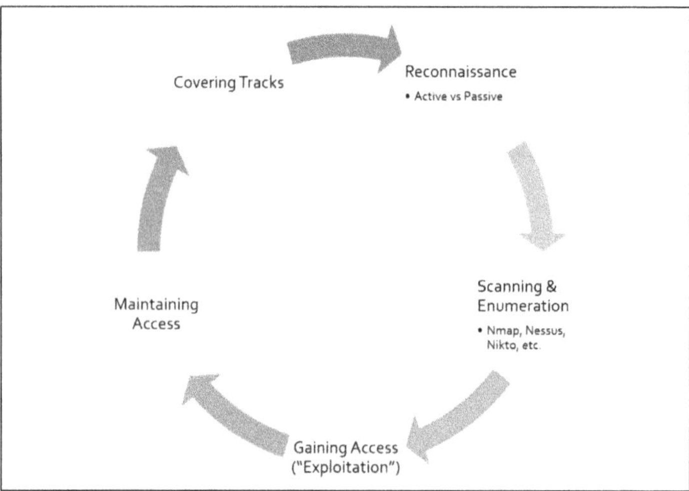

1. Reconnaissance:

This is the primary phase where the hacker tries to collect as much information as possible about the target. It includes identifying the target, finding out the target ip address range, network, domain name registration records of the target, mail server records, DNS records.

2. Scanning:

This makes up the base of hacking! This is where planning for attack actually begins! After reconnaissance the attacker scans the target for services running, open ports, firewall detection, finding out vulnerabilities, operating system detection.

3. Gaining Access:

After scanning the hackers designs the blueprint of the network of the target with the help of stuffs collected during phases one and 2! Now, the attacker, executes the attack based on the vulnerabilities which were identified during scanning! After the successful attack.he gets access to the target network!!!! So cool!! He is now, the king!!!

4. Maintaining Access:

After gaining access,the attacker escalates the privileges to root/admin and uploads a piece of code(usually called as backdoor) on the target network so that he always maintain the gained access and can connect to target anytime!

5. Covering Track:

After gaining access and maintaining the same, hacker exploits the weakness and hacks the network or misuses the access! After that, comes the important phase covering the tracks! To avoid getting traced and caught,hacker clears all the tracks by clearing all kinds of logs and deleted the uploaded backdoor and anything related stuff which may later reflect his presence! So these are five important phases of hacking which every hacker must follow for a successful attack!

Security and Privacy

We are all now well aware of the threats facing computers, such as DDoS attacks against servers, what exactly a zombie computer is and some hacks which have hit the newspapers - like the story of a man in Tampa Bay who was caught "stealing" someone else's broadband connection. The individual hacked into a wireless internet network.

While this may seem innocent enough consider that the person who gains entry into the network could be using your connection to surf for porn - or worse it could be child porn, with the trail leading to your connection.

In fact you may need to have your own experts helping you prove your innocence!

Another similar story of broadband/wireless signal theft from out of the UK, where several individuals have been charged using someone else's broadband connection.

While the fines have been hefty, it is a clear indication that while the justice system Is working towards protecting individuals, they are in uncharted territory. If you have ever borrowed someone else's wireless connection you should think twice. If the letter of the law is followed, you could end up with serious fines, jail time and worse, a record that will follow you for life.

If you have a wireless internet connection in your home, or office secure it! Not only are you protecting yourself, your business and its assets but you could be preventing someone from launching devastating attacks against commercial systems, or allowing terrorists from using open. systems to communicate with others and even stopping the flow of child pornography.

Forget about what could be done using your wireless connection consider that many of us store our entire lives on our computers: digital images, movies, banking information, and even e-bills. If someone gets unauthorized access to your computer, your risk having your identity stolen. You need to ensure your computer are sufficiently secured to prevent unauthorized access to its contents.

Best Hacking Tools

1. Nmap

Nmap allows you to scan your network and discover not only everything connected to it, but also a wide variety of information about what's connected, what services each host is operating, and so on. It allows a large number of scanning techniques, such as UDP, TCP connect (), TCP SYN (half-open), and FTP.
Nmap can be used by hackers to gain access to uncontrolled ports on a system. All a hacker would need to do to successfully get into a targeted system would be to run Nmap on that system, look for vulnerabilities, and figure out how to exploit them. Hackers aren't the only people who use the software platform, however.

2. Acutenix Web Vulnerability Scanner

Acunetix is an automated web application security testing tool that audits your web applications by checking for vulnerabilities like SQL Injection, Cross site scripting and other exploitable vulnerabilities. It also determines where applications need to be secured, thus protecting your business from hackers.

3.Metasploit

Metasploit is a penetration testing platform that simplifies the process of hacking. For several attackers and defenders, it is a must-have tool. Metasploit works flawlessly with Nmap, SNMP scanner, and Windows patch detection, among other tools, during the data gathering portion of a pentest.

FootPrinting

What is the first step one would take before seeking admission in a university or college? Quite unanimously, it must be a primary research about the institute.Footprinting is an analogous step which hackers take before gaining access into any network. The systematic foot printing of a organization enables attackers to create a complete profile of an organization's security posture like system architecture, network blocks and IP addresses exposed on the Internet. Hackers gain reconnaissance of the target following a sequence of steps as:

1 Open Source Footprinting- The first step a hacker takes is to visit the website of a potential target.He then looks for contact information of the administrators which may help in guessing the password or in Social Engineering.

1 Network Enumeration- This is the next step in gaining information where the hacker tries to identify the domain names and the network blocks of the target network.

1 Scanning- Once the network block is known, the next step is to spy for active IP addresses on the target network. The Internet Control Message Protocol (ICMP) is a good alternative for identifying active IP addresses.

People Searching

There are millions of or billions of searches conducted on a daily basis on all popular search engines as well as the popular social networking platforms. However what exactly these man search for is a matter of our concern. There are some platforms or tools that can be used to determine what exactly people search for on these search engines.

4 Steps People Use To Search

Pipl

What you will find when you visit Pipl is that this search engine does does not just search the web, but rather goes through searching an area this site refers to as the Invisible web. There are some hidden resources on the Internet that search engines simply can not or do not access for a variety of reasons. Some contains personal information, and the sites containing that information opt out of being indexed by the common search engines. Pipl is different because it does index such information.

What you can add will determine how exact your results may be. If you only have a name, you may get any information on anyone with that name. If you can add more, like a state, you are going to get more specific results.

Wink

Wink searches across what you would find using a regular search engine as well as across social communities, online profiles, etc. Some people searches work by looking for as many possibilities as possible, but Wink works in an almost opposite manner. Wink only searches for known information, so any advanced terms you enter need to be facts, like a birthday or city of birth about which you are certain. Possibilities will only confuse and limit unfairly your results. For this reason, Wink is particularly useful for those who know a lot of basic personal information about the person they are trying to find.

Facebook

Facebook is one of the world's largest social networks with hundreds of millions of people on this platform on a daily basis, it makes sense to use Facebook as an incredibly useful tool to find people online. This platform is used by billions of people over the world but only an few people know how to properly use this website. Facebook is often a widely used online networking program that allows peoples to share information with other people. You can even spy on peoples, find peoples working as an Artist, Singer, Professionals, etc. and contact them for your purpose.

PeekYou

PeekYou is an interesting twist to the world, it allows you to search for usernames across a variety of social networking PeekYou considers itself to be "The Smartest People Search Online." It is a website that brings people from all over the world together. Anyone with a PeekYou profile helps other people locate their websites, photos, social-networking pages, or any other contact information they have provided online.

Virtualbox For Hacking

Many of you have been having difficulty setting up your hacking environment to practice your hacks. In this chapter, I will show you the simplest and fastest way to set up an lab. to practice your hacks before taking them out into the real world where any slip-ups could be devastating.

Download VMware Workstation or Box

The best way to practice hacking is within a virtual environment. Essentially, you set up a hacking system, such as Kali Linux, and some victims to exploit. Ideally, you would want multiple operating systems (Windows XP, Vista, 7, and 8, as well as a Linux / Unix) and applications so that you can try out a variety of hacks.

Virtual machines and a virtual network are the best and safest way to set up a hacking lab. There are several virtualization systems out there, including Citrix, Oracle's VirtualBox, KVM, Microsoft's Virtual PC and Hyper-V, and VMware's Workstation, VMware Box, and ESXI. For a laboratory environment, I strongly recommend VMware's Workstation or Box.

Download Kali VMware Images

Once you have downloaded and installed your virtualization system, our next step is to the VMware images of Kali provided by Offensive Security, you won't have to create the virtual machine, but simply run it from Workstation or Box-This means that once you have downloaded the VM of Kali, you can then use it in either Workstation or Box without actually installing a new OS

Open Image with VMware

Once all the files have been unzipped, our next step is to the open this new virtual machine. Make note of the location where you have unzipped the virtual machine image. Then, go to either VMware Workstation or Box and go to File > Create new Machine > Allocate Ram & HDD Space > Select ISO File & Install the new OS in VMware

Download & Install Targets

For the next step, you need to download and install a target system. Of course, you could use your host Windows 7 or 8 system, but since this is practice, you might want to use an older, easier to hack system. Also, hacking your system can leave it unstable and damaged.

I recommend installing a Windows XP, Vista, Server 2003, or an older version of Linux. These systems have many known security flaws that you can practice on and, then when you become more proficient at hacking, and you can then upgrade to Windows 7 and 8 and newer versions of Linux.

If you or your friends don't have a copy of these older operating systems, you can purchase them very inexpensively many places on the Internet. Of course, you can also obtain these operating systems for free on many of the torrent sites, but BEWARE... you will likely be downloading more than just the operating systems. VERY often, these free downloads include rootkits that will embed in your system when you open the file.

Download Old Applications

Once you have your operating system in place, very often you will need applications to run on these older versions of the Windows and Linux operating systems. You will likely need a browser, Office, Adobe products, etc. These older. products have well-known security flaws that you can hone your skills on.

Reconnaissance

In the computer world, there are good guys who create networks that help us communicate, work with others and get information and then there are those not-so-good guys who, for a variety of reasons, like to use their computers to worm their way into those networks and cause trouble.

They're called hackers, and they'll routinely do things like:

- Steal secrets.
- Obtain passwords.
- Get credit card information.
- Create so much traffic that a website has to shut down.

Hackers are ALWAYS at work, either trying to steal information for their own gain or disrupt business as usual. You hear a lot of about hackers on the news now and then, but just what are they doing?

Here's a bit of background to help you understand what it means when a website or company is "hacked."
Hackers aren't heroes.

For some reason, there are those who think that hackers are "cool" and that their spirit of mischief and sneaking is admirable. But the IT (Information technology) experts who spend a lot of money building business or government networks would disagree. And, for that matter, so would anyone who has ever had their money or identity stolen by a hacker. There's nothing playful about that.

Most people would agree that there are three types of hackers:
- ➢ Young kids "having fun." These are adolescents who are essentially vandals on the Internet and are also know as Script Kiddies. They're not looking for more than few hours of their fun messing with websites or networks.
- ➢ A Recreational "hackers." These are savvy computer users who intrude on networks when they feel they have a valid reason to...in their minds at least. They may have a grudge against a certain website or company and take their dislike out by "hacking" or disrupting the website.
- ➢ Professionals. When a computer expert gets a taste of hacking and likes the flavor, he or she will continue to use their skill, often for breaking into people's accounts to steal money. They also might like taking down a big network for "fun."

Stealing passwords and getting in the system.

Finding out a password is the usually the first step in cracking a network's security. (That's why there are so many articles telling you to change your passwords often and make them hard to figure out!)

Here are a few key terms that you'll hear in discussions about hackers and what they do:

- **Backdoor.** A secret pathway a hacker uses to gain entry to a computer system.
- **Buffer overflow.** A method of attack where the hacker delivers malicious commands to a system by overrunning an application buffer.
- **Denial-of-service attack**. A attack designed to cripple the victim's system by preventing it from handling its normal traffic, usually by flooding it with false traffic.
- **Email worm**. A virus-laden script or mini-program sent to an unsuspecting victim through a normal-looking email message.
- **Root access**. The highest level of access (and most desired by serious hackers) to a computer system, which can give them complete control over the system.
- **Root kit.** A set of tools used by an intruder to expand and disguise his control of the system. Script kiddie. A young or unsophisticated hacker who uses base hacker tools to try to act like a real hacker.
- **Session hijacking**. When a hacker is able to insert malicious data packets right into an actual data transmission over the Internet connection.
- **Trojan horse**. A seemingly helpful program that tricks the computer user into opening it, only to deliver (unnoticed and behind the scenes) an unexpected attack on the user's computer.

VPN and TOR

VPN

VPN stands for "virtual private network" — a service that helps you stay private online. A VPN establishes a secure, encrypted connection between your computer and the internet, providing a private tunnel for your data and communications while you use public networks.

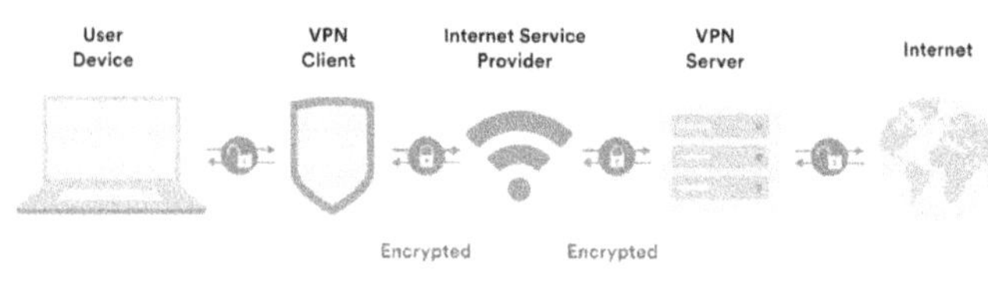

TOR

The Tor network is a secure, encrypted protocol that can ensure privacy for data and communications on the web. Short for the Onion Routing project, the system uses a series of layered nodes to hide IP addresses, online data, and browsing history.

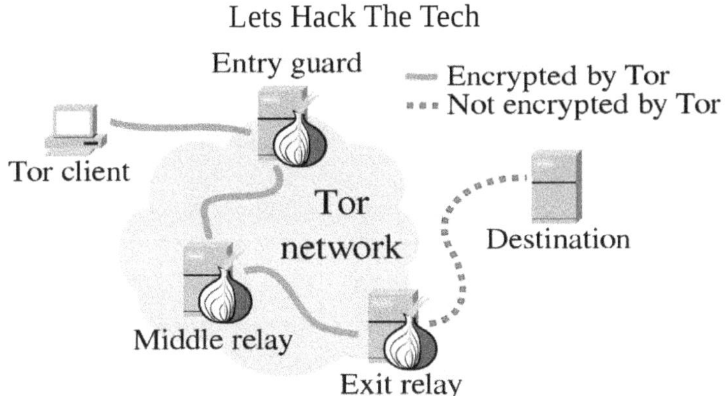

Using VPN and TOR

Using a proxy server is not completely secure, though. To communicate with your desired server providing the website you want to visit, the proxy has to decrypt your traffic and thus the internet provider of the proxy server is able to see the unencrypted data stream. This can be avoided by chaining proxies together or by simply using a service like Torwhichredirects your traffic through three proxies, so called "nodes." This way, it is almost impossible to identify you, but...

The 'big but' here is, that the exit node decrypts your traffic again to communicate with the server you are trying to reach, e.g. Google.com. This means that the exit node can easily spy on the contents of the packages you send through the tor network, like for instance unencrypted passwords and everything else which is not SSL encrypted. This can be used against you in many ways:

Absolutely everyone may provide a Tor node. The government, criminals, Although the exit node providers don't know who is sending

& requesting the traffic being redirected through their node, they can use the data they can "phish" this way against you anyway. Furthermore, it is pretty easy to figure out who you are by simply interpreting the recorded packages.

An alternative to Tor and similar services are VPN services. Same problem applies here: The VPN service provider can easily view your encrypted traffic & use it against you. It happened at least once that law enforcment infiltrated such a service and brought a whole organisation of internet criminals down.

The conclusion therefor is that such ways to remain anonymous might be efficient but you are always forced to trust the provider of the proxy/VPN service you want to use. In reality, this cannot be achieved. You do not know who is behind a service and even if this person can be trusted, he or she will not be allowed to tell you that the service is infiltrated by the government, not to mention the danger of such services being hacked.

Tips for Using VPN And Tor online (www.torproject.org)

A VPN or a virtual private network extends a particular private network across the public network and this includes the internet. It also enables the users to send as well as receive the data across the public networks and the shared networks. This is done as if they are computing devices and these devices are connected to the private network. A VPN is created by establishing a point to point connection by using various dedicated connections, traffic encryption and tunneling protocols. This is basically very much similar to the WAN that can also be called as a wide area network. You should follow these below tips to be a confident user of a VPN.

• Your firewall should be up and be running

This can sound a bit difficult and trivial. However a firewall should be on and running every time and it doesn't matter whether you are using a VPN or not, the firewall must be up and running 24 hours a day.

• You must stay incognito

Many people these days always forget that their browser can give away a huge amount of personal information. This mostly happens when the user is not using an incognito or a secure mode while using the website. There are also some websites that inform the user to go incognito when it is not secure and you as a user must need to do it.

•Disable all the geo- location services

Many of us are using smartphones and tablets for everyday use like Facebook and YouTube. All those who essentially want to use all these devices have to watch out for all the geo-location services and

• Manage all your cookies

These days no one in his or her busy life pays any attention to cookies. However these cookies are almost everywhere and this cookies often try to improve the recurrent browsing of the web. These cookies can very well be

transformed and modified into various tracking scripts and these can monitor your activity as well as the network information.

• The VPN over a TOR

TOR is probably a very big deal when this particular technology had come out and also an lot of us have used this TOR browser to use the Facebook at work. You can also rely on the TOR yourself. It is a very great and also an open source solution that is available for all the platforms. It is one of the important things to remember..

A VPN (Virtual Private Network) connects a PC or laptop over the Internet to the office network allowing the remote user to work as if they were sitting at their desk in the office. Normally, setting up a VPN requires significant technical skills as the office firewall needs to be reconfigured, the VPN server has to be setup and the whole lot has to be made secure. Once setup and working, the VPN server needs to be monitored (to ensure there is nothing suspicious going on) and maintained with the latest security patches provided by the VPN vendor.

However, there is an alternative way to setup a VPN by using a VPN service.A VPN service gives all the features of a VPN server but removes the complexity and cost of setup, monitoring and maintenance. To setup a VPN provided as a service, you need to visit the providers website, register online and download a piece of software to a system in the office network. This software connects the office network to the VPN Service via the Internet without having to change your firewall. By not changing your firewall, you have removed a potential attack point for hackers who scan firewalls to identify weaknesses. Once the office network is connected, you can then add users to the service and setup their PCs for VPN access. The more advanced VPN services provide a way to let the remote user set themselves up for access to the office so that within minutes of registering, a remote user can be working on their applications and files as if they were in the office.

Some hosted VPN services only provide access to a person's own PC which means that their office PC must always be powered on and that they have a PC/Laptop when out of the office. While these type of VPN services work, they are not very eco-friendly (you need a powered on PC for each remote user) and they don't support activities such as composing and reading mail when there is no internet access

Other VPN services connect the remote user to the office network as if their PC was on a very long cable. With these services a remote user connects directly to the file and mail servers without having to use a desktop PC. With this type of access, people use their laptop exactly the same way in and out of the office without having to remember if a file was stored on a server or on the laptop. Mail applications such as Microsoft Outlook work especially well on a network VPN as they allow the user to read and compose mail even when they are not connected to the VPN. When the user next connects to the VPN, outlook will automatically send all the newly created mail. Some VPN services will also provide a secure way to access mail and files from any web browser so that remote users do not need to have a laptop with them at all times.

Recommended VPN Providers

www.hidemyass.com

www.ipvanish.com

www.expressvpn.com

www.cyberghost.com

www.hsselite.com

Setting up VPN

Setting up a VPN can be done for various purposes such as for Remote Access over the Internet, Connecting Networks over the Internet and Connecting Computers over an Intranet. The aim of VPN is to provide the same services as that received through expensive leased lines, but at a lower. cost.

Here is a look at the step involved in setting up a VPN in your home computer. Select 'Control Panel' from the 'Start' menu. Here you need to select "Network and Internet Settings" and from here select 'Network Connections' in XP or the Network and Sharing Center in Vista. Proceed to complete the steps here by selecting 'Create a New Connection'. Next follow the upcoming steps till you complete the 'Allow Virtual Private Connections' step. Select the check box for each user that you want to give access over the VPN. This process completes the VPN setup. You can see new incoming connections at this point.

You need to visit a VPN service provider's website.Register online in the site and download the software to any system in the office network. This downloaded software establishes connection between the office networks with the VPN service through the internet without any need to change in the firewall. By leaving the firewall unchanged, the network is highly secured from the hackers. You can add users to the service once the office network is connected. The users can setup their computers for VPN access. There are advanced VPN service available, which allows the remote user to work immediately after registration. VPN service helps in limited hardware procurement and employing consultants to setup thus providing freedom to add or remove users at owner's requirement.

Change Or Spoof A Mac Address In Windows Or Os

Each Network Interface Card has a special MAC address. This applies to a wide range of system cards, including Ethernet cards and WiFi cards. The MAC Address is a six-byte number or 12-digit hexadecimal number that is utilized to remarkably distinguish a host on a system.

Different Ways Of Finding Your MAC Address

There are several ways of finding your Ethernet and communications protocol information. Many Ethernet card manufacturer's have proprietary software that can reveal this information, but they work differently depending on the manufacturer. So we will use the Windows 2000 and XP "ipconfig" utility since this is available in the majority of Windows Operating Systems.

First, go to "start" -> "run" and type "cmd" without the quotes. Then hit the enter key. At the command line type "ipconfig /all", again without the quotes. Actually, just typing ipconfig without the /all will work but will only provide you with abbreviated information regarding your network cards. An example of what you might see by typing the "ipconfig /all" command is below:

OutPut Of The "Ipconfig /All" Command

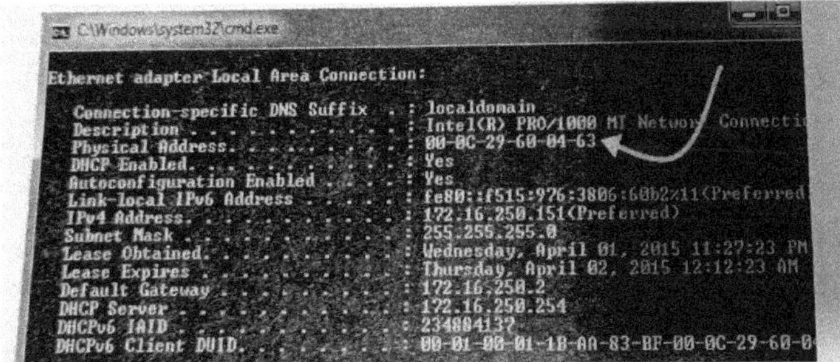

Recommended Tool for changing Mac Address

MacMakeUp - https://macmakeup.en.softonic.com/

MacMakeUp allows to changing MAC address to one of your choice or randomized one. Since first few symbols of MAC are code for hardware manufacturer app also has the internal list of those codes you can choose from.

There are some advanced settings, but I suggest they are not to be tinkered with unless you have good reason to. Same as with actual MAC address editing.

Malware

Malware is an often used, but seldom understood term that is used to generally describe malicious programs that identity thieves, hackers and Internet con-men use to control your computer and use it to perform tasks with you as the user often being none the wiser.

Malware includes all malicious programs ranging from annoying adware to the more dangerous spyware to the devastating impacts of computer viruses that can open up backdoors on your computer, allowing unknown third parties to control your computer as part of a zombie army to send spam, steal identity information and host illegal content on the Internet - - all under your name and online identity.

How Do You Become Infected?

Many malware applications are cleverly disguised as useful. even desirable pieces of software that the user mistakes as legitimate and blindly downloads onto their computer. For example, if a website offered you the opportunity to increase the speed of your internet for free, would you be tempted click 'download'? What about if you were offered a trial download of the world's "fastest and most secure" search engine for free?

In an ironic spin on this infection method, many malware applications are actually marketed as anti-malware tools and these are not backyard operations these - - are professional looking and highly deceptive websites that appear to offer legitimate products.

Malware also finds its way onto computers by piggy-backing off large, legitimate companies.For example, Firefox, the world's second most popular web browser has literally thousands of endorsed and homebrew extensions - some of which may contain malware. Toolbars, messenger extensions and screensavers are all favourite hiding places of dangerous malware applications.

Malware is also commonly installed onto a system through Active-X controls: special programs that can change your computer's registry and literally take control of particular computer functions. While Active-X controls can be dangerous, they are also used legitmitely for many different uses. Too often users find themselves infected with malware just by being too trusting and clicking 'Accept' just too quickly.

Malware can be launched from almost any web link, image or video, meaning that social networking sites like Facebook and Google+ are literal breeding grounds for malware applications as videos and images 'go viral', infecting huge numbers of linked computers very quickly.

What Does Malware Do?

As mentioned before, the functions of malware range from annoying to devastating. Some of the most common functions off malware include:

The collection and transmission of personal details, account information and passwords back to an unknown third party server,

Serving the user with unwanted and persistent advertising,

If a user enters an incorrect web address, the browser can redirect them to a commercial or compromising website,

The user's homepage can be hijacked and changed to a commercial or phishing website,

Changing a web-browser's security settings and operating function, making it easier for security to be compromised,

Diminishing the overall performance of the user's computer before redirecting them to a registry cleaning product or system enhancer.

Malware and spyware are certainly real threats for anyone using a computer that is connected to the Internet. Malware is any program with a purpose of infiltrating a computer without user knowledge of the infection with the purpose to damage the system, steal information, or just be annoying to the user. Spyware is a specific type of malware which is characterized by the intent to steal personal information. from a user. Computer users have to take the offensive when it comes to keeping their systems clean from infections while surfing the Internet. A combination of keeping the latest patch levels on both Windows updates as well as virus scan signature updates in conjunction with being vigilant when it comes to the types of sites a user visits and makes themselves available to will greatly reduce the odds of infection. Malware can be a tremendous threat to Internet users. Malware software presents itself in a number of ways and in many cases, it damages a computer to the point where a user simply has to reload the operating system. The results can be:

• Corrupted files

• Stolen personal information including credit card numbers. bank accounts,etc
• Annoying pop up ads that a user remove
• Software that cannot be uninstalled by conventional means
• Passing the infection along to other users

There are five types of malware out there today

(1) Contagious Software. This type of software is composed of computer viruses or so-called worms. This type of malware is the most common. A "virus" describes a computer virus rather than an actual physical virus which may infect us. Viruses are different than worms in their distribution and the actual operation.

The first type of malware to evolve was the computer virus. Viruses work and spread within the infected system by attaching themselves to other software. In the case of macro viruses, to documents. During the execution of the program, the viral code is executed. Viruses spread across computers when the software or document they attached themselves to is transferred from computer to computer.

The computer worm, used to infect systems, began when the internet was first used.The worm scans different networks in the computer, testing for any vulnerable systems where it can copy itself. From this new base, inside your computer the worm begins scanning and copying itself to all vulnerable files or processes. Although worms and viruses had distinct meanings and uses, they now are used to indicate any type of contagious malware.

Computer worms are stand-alone software and thus do not require other pieces of software to attach themselves to. They are started as part of the boot process. Worms spread, either by exploiting some vulnerability of the target system, or by using some kind of social engineering to trick users into executing them.

(2) Hidden files. This type of malware is used to hide any type of activity within a user's computer. There are various types of hidden files, such as:

(a) A Trojan. These are the familiar trojan horses. They serve the same purpose as the mythical trojan horse. You know, the one the Greeks used to take over Troy. Some trojans are registered on your computer in the form of utilities. When the user downloads the malware, a door opens for other types of malware to be introduced into the system.

Trojan horses are get executed by being part of an otherwise useful piece of software. Trojan horses are attached to the host software manually, they cannot infect other pieces of software the way viruses can, nor can they replicate themselves. Trojan horses rely on the useful features of the host software, which trick users to install them. One of the most insidious types of Trojan horse is a program that claims to rid your computer of viruses but instead introduces viruses into your computer. The devious mind that creates the virus and plants it successfully will see a massive computer outbreak of the virus. By introducing the virus into one network via a trojan horse, the creator sees the spread of the virus to other networks.

(b) A Backdoor. A Backdoor is a piece of software that allows access to the computer system, bypassing the normal authentication procedures. This virus creates an alternative doorway inside your structure. It creates a different pathway or route to the goodies. This virus circumvents any security system residing on your computer. Once inside the system via the backdoor, the hacker will be able to do anything they want to do.

There are two groups of backdoors. The first group works much like a Trojan. They are manually inserted into another piece of software, executed via their host software and spread by their host software being installed. The second group works more like a worm in that they get executed as part of the boot process and are usually spread by worms carrying them as their payload.

(3) For Profit Malware. There are some disreputable companies out there who will increase their profits any way they can. This malware comes in the form of a dialer. A dialter is the type of malware which goes through your internet connection, rerouting your net connections through an expensive phone line. This increases your bill that you have to pay.A computer that has this malware is forced to call the compliant phone line and run up a huge bill.

(4) An Exploit. A piece of software that attacks a particular security vulnerability. Exploits are not necessarily malicious in intent - they are often devised by security researchers as a way of demonstrating that a vulnerability exists. However, they are a common component of malicious programs such as network worms.

(5) Phony or Hoax Viruses. There are instances where hoay virus warning messages have been sent which suggest that the recipient may have a particular virus, together with helpful instructions about how to confirm and eliminate the virus. These messages almost invariably tell you to look for a particular file and if it is present, delete it. In most cases, the file which they mention is a Windows system file which if deleted will cause serious running problems.

Hackers, Hoaxes And Spyware

Everyone who has an ISP, understands, or at least knows about how hackers use viruses, Trojans, and other web nasties, to infect and mess up your computer. No headline news there. (Unfortunately, we still don't understand why they do it, or at least I don't.) But hackers don't have to write malicious code or hijack your browser to do some serious damage to your system. Oh no... A well written email with no attachments can do the trick. They only have to start a rumor.

Hackers can easily manipulate you into trashing your own computer. All they have to do is begin a hoax.
Hoaxes work incredibly well for getting average people to cause their own computers to malfunction. The hacker doesn't have to spend any time creating malicious code and a method of distribution, all they have to do is play on the human tendency for hysteria; send out a warning that something evil is spreading, and if you find it on your computer, get rid of it!

Recently I was tracking a thread on a forum, where the moderator warned everyone about a file that he found on his system that was a keylogger. (A keylogger is a malicious program designed to track your every move through monitoring your keystrokes.) He warned everyone to search for a file, ans2000.ini and, "delete the booger."

Hoaxes are just as dangerous as live viruses, because they inspire you to destroy your own programs. I am sure they are a particular kick for the one starting the hoax, as they are getting you to do bad things to your own system. Fear is a powerful motivator, and hoaxes, by design, are created to cause panic and fear in the less experienced Internet traveler.

So, before going and deleting files from your hard drive, go check them out. Do a search for them and read the information you find. Don't just go deleting things without learning about them first, or you just may end up cutting your own throat. And, NEVER forward these types of warning emails to others until you know for a fact that the information is correct, or you're likely to have your friends and family after you for misinforming them.

Eliminating Spyware, Adwares, and Viruses

Preventing Malicious Processes from Getting Installed:

Do not download all kinds of random stuff!

For example, it's OK to download a picture (by right clicking it and choosing "Save Picture As") from a website. There is no harm in this, generally. However, downloading screensavers and "free" games and other supposedly free software constantly is not good. It doesn't mean all free stuff is bad, just be careful only to download free programs from sites you trust (big name sites are often a good choice).

It's also OK to open a attachment from a friend you trust, but avoid opening and reading email forwards, especially if they have attachments! Email forwards start with "FW:"-ask friends who send forwards not to send them, as you do not open or read them anyway. Forwards are arguably a waste of time and ones with attachments are not worth the risk.

When you download and install a program, don't just click Next or Yes when the installation prompts you with options. Uncheck boxes with toolbars and other add-ons that you may not want.

Don't just install things when prompted while surfing the net!

When, a website says, "This site wants to install bla," make sure it's a site you trust and that you REALLY NEED whatever you are trying to access. For example, if you are on a major broadcasting company's site trying to watch a video, it's obviously ok. If you are on some unknown site trying to get something, think twice.

If you weren't trying to get anything at all, definitely click the red X in the corner! Never click Yes or No, just click the Red X. If that doesn't work, press ALT+F4 on your keyboard to close the site!

Eliminating Things Manually

Stop unneeded processes!

Press CTRL+ALT+DEL (all at once) and see what is running in the Processes tab. See something you don't recognize? Google it. If it's not needed, you'll want to end it by right clicking it and choosing End Process. Do this any time your system acts up. Go through the list and see if anything weird is there, then Google it. (NOTE: Don't end something unless you are sure it is not needed!)

Control what runs when Windows starts up!

Click START, go to RUN and type msconfig, then click OK. Choose selective startup and go to the Startup tab. Anything you don't recognize here? Google it. If it's not necessary, uncheck the box. Go through the whole list and do this, then click OK and restart when you are ready. After rebooting, Windows will remind you that you've chosen selective startup.

Social Engineering

Children's seem like they understand how to apply the concept of social engineering Children makes lots of noise with promise of being quiet only when they get the toy or trip they want. People are also manipulated psychologically until they do what hackers wants such as give up personal or confidential information online and offline. Like DDoS (distributed denial of service) is usually one of many components of a blueprint with goals of extortion, system or network access, bribery, bullying, identity theft, business destruction, human and drug trafficking, and other types of fraud and illegal activity. On the flip side, these social engineering and hacking combination of activities may have a goal of "remedying a perceived social inequity" or achieving scientific research.

Some say that Kevin Mitnick, once known as the world's most wanted hacker, is the one who first coined the term "social engineering." The phrase has a bad reputation online, but whether it is a good or bad activity is in mind of the beholder just as DDoS, phone pranks, and other activities that may social engineering attack online and offline. Every time a woman or an man does anything in the attempt to get others to do what she or he wants, that is social engineering

Again, social engineering is the act of duping an individual into revealing information that should be confidential or into doing something he or she would not normally do. The victims of such are not necessarily gullible or ignorant. Maybe it is just that they trust practically everyone.They enjoy helping others. On the other hand, the perpetrators of social engineering are appealing to universal, time-resistant human desires and emotions: lust, friendship, power, luck, money, greed, revenge, charity, accomplishment, fame, and being a part of a bigger cause. Perpetrators can easily trick people into giving up information that they have no idea is destined to compromise a server, computer, business, family, network, or other online or offline person, place, thing, idea or organization.

Hacking is the act of entering a computer system via a security breach; whereas, social engineering is as an invasion of the mind. Have you heard of emotional intelligence? People with keen emotional intelligence make great social engineers and can make unbelievable things happen just as computer system hackers can. Combine the two and discover potentially unstoppable collaborations that can wreak painful havoc, insane genius, unbelievable change-making or huge accomplishment for organizations and individuals online and offline. Sounds had, doesn't it?However, the two are combined throughout history for good and evil, depending upon your point of view.

Social Engineering Expert: Hacker's Greatest Tool

It is the art of manipulating people into doing something, like divulging confidential information or performing actions that would expose information, and making them feel good about doing it, I.e they "solved" a problem or helped someone, etc. This allows the hacker to obtain information in a no threatening manner. Let us now explore some examples how easy it is for a hacker to utilize social engineering to obtain confidential or sensitive information.

There are several examples where social engineering can be used for personal gain, other than divulging information One very common example that is employed by many people on a frequent basis: paying a compliment to the hostess a fine restaurant thinking you may be seated at a nicer table or seated faster, or doing the same to your waiter or waitress to get faster service. at a

All too often in today's society, social engineering is being used for dubious reasons, so a hacker can obtain sensitive personal and/or company information. This has now become a real threat to the security of your employees, confidential client information, and company records and/ banking information.

Here are some of the social engineering tricks and scams:

The IT Support Person Scam:

The social engineer gains access to your computer systems by calling as an IT support person. Generally, this is easier to do when there is a lot of buzz about a virus or malware in the media. It can, however, happen at any time. The person posing as IT support (the imposter) calls a user and attempts to lead them through some sort of fix for the malware. The imposter continues to stress how important fixing this is and causes the end user to become frustrated. Once the user becomes frustrated, the imposter says something along the lines of "Let's save us both time. Why don't you give me your password, I'll deal with the problem and call you back."

A variant of this scam, with some additional twists, has been used to take significant amounts of money (six figures in this case) from a law firms bank accounts.

Jury Duty or Subpoena Scam:

The phone rings in the early evening. The caller states the person answering the phone has failed to report for jury duty, or appear as required by a subpoena. This usually takes the answerer by surprise. The caller then asks for the answerer's full name, social security number, and date of birth, so they may "verify" they are the person who failed to appear. The unsuspecting readily supplies this information and ends up becoming the victim of identity theft.

The Foreign Traveler Scam:

This generally happens when a hacker gains access to a email account or a Facebook account. The hacker then uses the account to send a bogus email or Facebook posts to the real account owners contacts. The post reads something like this:

Subject: "Predicament (Sad news)!!!".

Email Body: "I feel terrible disturbing you with this, but I don't had any other option. I had to travel to Alaska for something urgent but now I am in a tight situation here. Pleased your help with a loan of $1800 to sort myself out. I will refund you immediately when I return this weekend. If you can help with this let me know so I can tell you how to get it to me.

Click this to send funds.

Thanks, Becky"

Of course, Becky's close friends would hate to see Becky stuck in a foreign country so they will click a link and follow the instructions to send money to "Becky". The bank will look like a legitimate bank website (Chase or Bank of America) fooling even the most observant individuals. It will ask Becky's saviors to send funds to her via a bank account setup in her name in that foreign country.

Disaster Relief Scam:

This scam usually happens right after a disaster such as a hurricane or has happened most recently the bombing at the Boston Marathon. Fake donation sites appear on the internet by the hundreds or even thousands. The purpose of these sites is to use the emotional appeal of helping victims to capture credit card or bank account information from those who are well meaning, and would like to help. We definitely encourage those who wish to help in these situations, BUT, check out the website and the foundation set up before you donate.

Free Gift cards or Airline Tickets:

This type of threat happens often via email on Facebook, Tumblr, and Pinterest. The user is prompted with an "ad" that indicates that the user will receive a free gift card or software upgrade or perhaps even some of Bill Gates fortune, for filling in a survey. Stay away!!! These companies are not really giving away anything They are merely collecting information from the unsuspecting that can be used to steal an Identity.

Unauthorized Access to Your Building or Offices:

Typically someone will be hanging out in a smoking area and chatting it up with fellow smokers who have access to a secure building or office. When the real employees go to enter the facility, the imposter merely follows them using a technique called "tailgating. If the employees ask the imposter for their ID, access card, or badge, the imposter will simply tell the employees they left their access card in their office. "Cigarettes, a Social Engineer's best friend."

Another way of gaining unauthorized access to your building or offices is for the "imposter' to have lots of packages or simply say "I'm in a hurry, please let me in".

Social Engineering is here to stay. If it sounds too good to be true or employees feel something just doesn't feel right, they should trust their gut instinct. Odds are unless you are vigilant, you will not know you are a victim until it is too late. It is very important to have a stated IT policy in place, as well as a safety policy, and to have your employees familiar with both of them. The more aware they can be the less likely you, your employees, or your company will become the victim or an unwilling hacker.

Ways To Use Public Wi-Fi to Hack Identity

1. Man-in-the-Middle Attacks

The technological term, man-in-the-middle (MITM) is an attack whereby a third party intercepts communications between two participants. Instead of data being shared. directly between server and client, that link is broken by another element. The uninvited hijacker then presents their own version of a site to display to you, adding in their own messages.

Anyone using public Wi-Fi is especially vulnerable to an MITM attack. Because the information transmitted is generally unencrypted, it's not just the hotspot that's public it's your data too. You might as well shout out your details. A compromised router can vacuum up a lot of personal material relatively simply: just getting into your emails, for instance, gives hackers access to your usernames, passwords, and private messages.

2. Fake Wi-Fi Connections

This variation of an MITM attack is also known as the "Evil Twin". The technique intercepts your data in transit, but bypasses any security systems a public Wi-Fi hotspot might have. The trouble caused by connecting to a malicious router. In that case, users were integrated into an alien intelligence admittedly unlikely. But in reality, victims could be handing over all their private information, merely because they were tricked into joining the wrong network.

It's fairly easy to set up a fake access point (AP), and is well worth the effort for cybercriminals. They can use any device with internet capabilities, including a smartphone, to set up an AP with the same name as a genuine hotspot. Any transmitted data sent after joining a fake network goes via a hacker.

3. Packet Sniffing

It's an amusing name, but the actual practice of "packet sniffing" is far from a laughing matter. This method enables a hacker to acquire airborne information then analyze it at their own speed. A device transmits a data packet across an unencrypted network, which can then be read by free software like Wireshark. That's right: it's free. Look online and you'll even see "how to" guides, teaching you how to use Wireshark. Why? Because it's a handy tool for analyzing web traffic, including, ironically enough, finding cybercriminals and vulnerabilities that need patching.

4. Session Hijacking

Sidejacking relies on obtaining information via packet sniffing. Instead of using that data retroactively, however, a hacker uses it on-location. Even worse, it bypasses some degrees of encryption! Log-in details are typically sent through an encrypted network (hopefully) and verified using the account information held by the website. This then responds using cookies sent to your device. But the latter isn't always encrypted - a hacker can hijack your session and can gain access to any private accounts you're logged into.

5. Shoulder-Surfing

Whenever using an ATM, you should check those around you, making sure no one's peeking as you enter your PIN. It's also a danger when it comes to public Wi-Fi. If one or more individuals are hovering around when you're visiting private sites, stay suspicious. Don't submit anything personal like a password. It's a very basic scam, but one that certainly still works for hustlers and hackers.

Spy Software

Most computers now of days come equipped with some sort of junk software that tries to help keep your computer safe from viruses or what ever may want to creep onto your computer. The fact is these software's are low end, pieces of junk that really need to be tossed. What should I do to keep my computer safe, and protected? Well the software isn't the flaw, it's the type of spy software that your purchase. Purchasing the right software is a big decision, and must be done right. It could potentially protect you from losing credit card information or even your identity.

So what's a good spy software you ask? Below I will list the top 5 softwares available on the market today. Each and every software has it's pros and cons. We will start at the top with number one being the best and five being the worst.

1. SpyAgent:

Spy Agent is a full featured PC and Internet activity monitoring software that enables you to record everything on your PC. This product is extremely stealth and packs a big punch.

2. RealtimeSpy:

This software has more features than any remote software product we've reviewed and is strongly recommended. Realtime spy offers the best remote monitoring solutions.

3. SpyAnywhere:

SpyAnywhere provides the power to remotely control computers with SpyAnywhere installed all from your favorite web browser! This remote monitoring tool is excellent for PC users.

4. Keystroke Spy:

Keystroke Spy is a cost effective monitoring solution that allows you to easily and efficiently log what your computer users are doing. This is a affordable yet powerful tool for home users. 5. Sentry PC:

Sentry PC is the perfect choice for parental control and monitoring of your child's activities. The software enables you to restrict access, filter and monitor your children's activity.

Spy Devices

When people have problems like cheating spouse and unruly children, exercising strictness and severity will only harm their relationship rather than doing any good. So what should be done in such a scenario? Well, one pertaining solution is to bring into play spy phone software which actively spy on their activities without their knowledge. Novices, who are inexperienced in working with the mobile phone spy, more often than not have the predicament whether or not the spy devices work perfectly.

The answer to this quandary is a definite affirmative as you do not require knowing biomedicine and rocket science to make use of cell phone spy software. Mobile spy can help you keep a tab on the activities of your cheating spouse and can effectively save your marriage from ruining itself to ground.

In these times of advanced technologies and state of the art contrivances, you can utilize spy phone software to its full potential and the ones you are using on, will never know of the thing that you are spying on them. This spy bug will also help you as SMS spy as you will be able to read their text messages. The sheer volume and amount of information you will be able to acquire through the GSM spy will surely sweep you off your feet.

If you doubt a scenario of cheating spouse, you can always read their secret messages and listen to what they are saying. The mobile phone spy or cell phone spy will surely astonish you to your wit's end when you reckon its super abilities. The World Wide Web is the best place to search for pertaining spy phone software and other spy devices. With a bit of intricate research on the internet, you will be able to lay your hands on precise and pertinent information on cell phone spy and other spy phone. Its capability to turn any mobile phone into a high end surveillance contrivance makes it just the more alluring and lucrative.

The time tested and trustworthy features of a spy phone will surely astound you by the results it endows you with. One can integrate in the victim's phone hardware and rest assured that it is utterly undetectable. Let us sneak a quick look through some of the advantages of this spy phone software: - first of all since it is based on a cellular network, you can avail nearly endless span of transmission, wherein tapping cell phone calls, receiving SMS copy is utterly straight forward and without any glitches.

These spy devices are hidden in a phone's hardware and are irremovable and undetectable. Even if someone changes the SIM or replace the phone number, you would still be able to gain information from the new number. There are features wherein you can remotely lock down the device without interrupting any spy features which are active. There is a master phone which controls the spy phone and all the activities of the spy phone can be saved in the master phone for future references.

Spy Pen

Most of us are aware of what a spy pen is, a camera that is created and squeezed into a pen for the purpose of discreet recording. But most of us a blissfully unaware of the technology that goes into making these spy cameras so independent of any other device. DVR, short for Digital Video Recording, is the future of these devices and allows us to enhance the quality and accessibility of our recorded footage.

Spy Pen digital video recorders normally record in the .avi or .3gp file formats, these are excellent and widely supported formats by not only PC's and Macs but cell phones, and 95% of the variations of DVR players on the market.

Digital Video is the only format that files can be shared over the web. Many people are now opting to stream footage live to other locations all over the world. DVR has made this possible. By setting up a live transmission feed from the spy pen camera you can get the file streamed directly to a server on the internet which is easy to view from any device with internet access.

DVR is now available on both audio and video spy pens, so high quality recording options are open to you regardless of the type of spy pen you wish to purchase.

Another great quality of DVR recordings is that they are easy to manipulate at a later time. Many pieces of software on a pc can open the files and manipulate the code to enhance certain parts of aspects of the recorded track.

The most widely selling spy camera pens is the 4gb spy pen DVR recorder; this spy pen will record up to 4-6 hours worth of footage. Which is quite amazing for such a tiny camera, the DVR components allow you to stop and start the footage recording multiple clips or leave it running for one super clip.

Despite this, there is a distinct advantage to the DVR pen or any other spy pen that is battery like. Because the device is so small it con only contain a limited size battery. Most models these days include a stationary non-removable battery which charge when you plug the pen into another electrical device, much like many cell phones.

Even the best of these batteries will only manage to record for 3-4 hours before shutting down; this greatly limits the potential of even a great recording method such as the DVR.

Spying in Shades:

Imagine this scene if you can.Inside a very busy airport, exchange between terrorists and gunrunners is taking place. The deal does not go unnoticed or unmonitored by several countries' intelligence bureaus. In fact, agents are swarming all over the airport, all of them in various disguises. One of them goes undercover as a teenager.He sports very dark, very sleek sunglasses.He strikes conversation with one of the terrorists. Unbeknownst to the terrorist, the agent is recording his features, physique, voice, and movement. How? Through a video recorder implanted in the agent's sunglasses. a a

Does this scene seem like something plucked right out of a James Bond flick? Yes, it does. Reality, however, has finally caught up with fiction. Today, you need not be a member of the secret service just to wear spy camera glasses. Many companies are manufacturing spy camera glasses.In fact, these are available on and off the Internet.

Spy Camera Glasses What?

Spy camera glasses look no different from regular eyewear. They are so innocuous-looking, in fact, they would seem identical to the spectacles your grandfather has on, or the shades your sister frequently dons.

Spy camera glasses are designed for covert operations. They are particularly useful in espionage and law enforcement. Authorities uses them to obtain information or put suspects under surveillance. Spy camera glasses also come handy to private detectives who use them to catch erring spouses or obtain damaging evidence for use in litigations.

How Do Spy Camera Glasses Work?

How is it possible to record someone using sunglasses? Well, mankind has made such dramatic strides in miniaturization we now have cameras so small they can easily be concealed in an eyewear's nosepiece. In spy camera glasses, the camera concealed in the nose piece may either be wired or wireless. The camera records the information and then transmits the same either in color or in black and white.

Going Wireless

Wireless spy camera glasses are powered by batteries. These batteries, however, are different from the type we often buy for our portable radios. They are so long-lasting they can. keep the hidden video camera running for long periods of time.This feature of spy camera glasses is important. After all, anyone who's ever done any surveillance work can tell you your worst enemy is time. There's no telling how long you'd have to wait for your quarry to emerge from the office, for example, or head for his paramour's house.

Staying Wired

Now, what of wired spy camera glasses? They have thin wires connecting the camera to a transmitter or recording device. This transmitter or recording device can be easily kept inside a jeans pocket.

Clearly, mankind has come a long way from the days of yore. Not only have we leaped from caves to mansions, we have now produced eyewear capable of performing as video. cameras. Spy camera glasses are marketed so widely, in fact, you can buy one yourself. Whether you need it for legitimate reasons or you just think it's cool to own one, you can spy in your shades anytime, anywhere.

Overview Of Automation Industry

What is Automation?

In general, automation is achieved by various means including electrical, computers, pneumatic, hydraulic and mechanical (usually in combination).Airplanes, ships, and factories use all these combined topics.

Benefits of Automation

Saves labor time

Saves energy and materials

Higher productivity

Better control and consistency Improves quality

Increase efficiency

Improves accuracy

Eliminate human errors

Increase flexibility

Saves workers from hazardous environment

Disadvantages of Automation

Poses security threats

Excessive development costs

Higher initial cost Higher level of maintenance

Worker displacement due to loss of jobs to machines

Over dependency on technology for productivity & economic development.

Why Business Needs Automation?

In this hyper competitive world, every business has to scale up continuously to keep up and stay ahead in the race. To Improve the processes, reduce costs, increase productivity, Improve efficiency & accuracy, etc. business houses need automation.

Why Automation Training is Important?

Automation training helps a professional to develop skill sets and improve efficiency to tackle real world challenges. It prepares a student or an employee with requisite capabilities to meet changing market demands and get ready for future challenges. Automation training upgrades a trainee's skills as per industry trends and clients' specific demands and requirements.It also exposes a student to various usage scenarios in the automation industry in advance. Equipping oneself with automation training enables a student or a professional to join the best companies in the automation industry and opens up various career opportunities.

Scope of Employment in Automation Sector

Automation is a fast growing field and there are huge opportunities for automation engineers. An automation engineer can work in three kinds of companies -

1) Companies which are suppliers of automation software and equipment to multiple industries

2) Industries like automotive, oil & gas and power which uses automation products and services 3) Companies which offer consultancy and services, who integrate products from automation companies with manufacturing processes of the industrial users

There are two types of companies that recruit freshers or experienced engineers. The first type of companies are hardcore electronic or electrical firms e.g.Siemens which hire for design, projects, commissioning, engineering, servicing and sales of the automation products and services. Here the automation products and services could be networking systems, Sensors. The second type of firms are manufacturing or consumer industries, where automation engineers are required. Firms such as Iron & Steel etc. belong to the consumer industries.

Automation is reducing the need for people in many jobs.Computers and robots have made remarkable advances into the workforce in recent years, not only on the factory floor but also in law offices, banks and motor vehicles. Not that it's the first time technology has replaced humans in the workplace. Mechanical looms took the place of artisans 200 years ago. The rise of personal computers reduced the need for secretaries 30 years ago. These advances in automation took a toll on specific professions and industries but raised our living standards overall.

The difference today is that changes seem to be coming much faster than before. We live in a time of exponential growth in technology. While most high-skill jobs requiring problem-solving and creativity are safe, and many low-skill jobs seem resilient to automation, Autor thinks middle-skill jobs like machinists and bookkeepers are most at risk.

Still, while automation and robotics have made tremendous advances for example, Siri's language interface and Google's driverless car are two milestones many thought would not be met this quickly -- there are large hurdles that preclude robots' world domination. While robots are highly efficient at applying math to do routine tasks, humans are able to complement their robot "colleagues" with non programmable capabilities, such as the ability to be flexible and adaptable, interact effectively with humans, and use judgment and common sense to solve unexpected problems.

Examples of Automation in IT Sector

- ➤ Chat Bots – Providing customer support to users with automated scripts

- ➤ Form Filling – Automation has become so advance that it can even fill up the forms itself and submit Technical Support

- ➤ Making Money – Yes it's true you can make a lot of money with automation just you need to think the right steps for automation tool to follow

- ➤ Any online/offline task on computer – You can have automation for both browsers and windows, any task which includes just repeated work and some conditions which can be coded.

Game Hacking

The title of most important and significant discovery of this millennium can rightly fully be bestowed upon the invention of Computers. The advent of computers has made a positive impact on every aspect of our daily lives. From speeding up mundane everyday office tasks such as word processing to carrying out a complex and life on the line heart surgery, computers make the process smooth, speedy and virtually error free.

Even the most well made and highly ranked games developed by the most reputable developers are prone to glitches. These glitches could be in rare cases beneficial to a gamer and in most cases are big nuisances to deal with. Game glitches section is put up by people who have encountered these glitches while playing a particular video game and want to share it with rest of community. Now game glitches could exist as a separate section or be a part of the game blog; it tells about specific glitches like absence of texture, hanging frame rates or faulty Al about a game.

If the game glitches are fixable with minor tweaks, it is generously mentioned by the players for the benefit of others in the community or else alternate ways are mentioned to overcome the problem.

In some cases, a gamer feels the urge to turn certain aspects of the game in his/her favor or according to his/her liking. It might be that some part of the game is a bit too generically difficult to overcome and is frustrating the player; in such cases, a seasoned gamer usually consults game hacking articles on the internet. Although, game hacking is not officially recommended as it could corrupt the game, but that does not stop the community from altering the game source code to suit their own needs and requirements.

PSP Game Hack

Many PSP fans, including myself, are already looking for ways to push their PSP's to the extreme. I want more options, more PSP games, and a whole cinema full of PSP Movies.

Here's a great example; many PSP fans are old gamers of the past and since hauling around your old super nintendo is out and totally nerdy... here's what you can do:

Search the web for a PSP Game Emulator.

Game Emulator

Ah, that is the secret to a world of PSP fun. Real simply a PSP Game Emulator is software that lets your PSP pretend that is another type of game console. So you can load up games from say your PlayStation 3 and play them on your Sony PSP.

Hack Slash Crawl is an action RPG game much like the recently released Torchlight. You go around slaying goblins while at the same time, you're upgrading your weapons and armor in order to fight more menacing enemies along the way.

There's no story to this game unlike with console-based RPGs. As you start the game you're already transported inside a dark and depressing dungeon expected slay pretty much everything that moves. The controls are fairly easy to master since everything is controlled by the click of a mouse.

To move all you have to do is highlight a area using the mouse and click. It's fairly simple although it can get a bit tedious sometimes if you're trying to move away from baddies all the time. But the easiest thing about the game is combat.

There are no complex controls for you to memorize as your character automatically fights enemies that you highlight over with the mouse. As long as the enemy is in range of the main character, he will keep fighting until everyone around him is dead. The only way to stop him from fighting is to simply run away.

It's advisable that you use this technique because some areas there are time where the enemy can overwhelm you in big numbers. They can surround you and even chase you for several meters! Don't worry you can eventually get your revenge as this game has arguably the best feature ever in an RPG game that is a recoverable health bar.

Android Rooting

Andriod Rooting means of unlocking the operating system so you can install unapproved apps, deleted unwanted bloatware, update the OS, replace the firmware, overclock (or underclock) the processor, customize anything and so on.

Of course, for the average user, this sounds like -- and can be -- a scary process. After all, "rooting" around in your smartphone's core software might seem like a recipe for disaster. One wrong move and you could end up with bricked handset.

Android is a very versatile, customizable and open operating system. You may think that rooting is not for you, but it can actually help you to a very great extent. With so little work, so much can be achieved. You may have heard bad things about rooting but in some cases, you may consider using it, especially if it is done by people, who are aware of what needs to be done. Some of the reasons include:

1. Features and apps

Rooting helps you to get the features that you want. There are times when an app may be blocked by different carriers or may hack into the system files or may be unavailable. Rooting assists with this making the apps that had been incompatible previously to be compatible. Rooting gives you the chance to do so much more with your gadget.

2. Automation

There are apps that one can use so as to automate everything on the phone. If you root, then there is so much more that you will discover. Some tasks like turning on the screen, changing speed of the CPU, toggling GPS and 3G all require rooting. When you want to reap the full benefits of some apps, then it is totally necessary to root.

3. Boosting the speed and battery life

There is so much more that can be done if at all you need to boost battery life and also speed up the phone even if you do not root. However, if you do root, you get so much more power. There are apps that you can use to overclock or under clock the phone so as to have greater performance. You can use yet others apps, so as to hibernate some of the apps that aren't in use.

4. Blocking ads in apps

Ads can be very irritating and they actually use up your data. If you want the ads blocked in devices and apps, then rooting can actually help to a great extent. There are various options that you can pursue if your phone is rooted.

5. Backing up the transitions

When you change devices or when the device is restored, you can back up the apps and the settings. In this way, it becomes easier to get the setups. There are things that can be backed up without rooting.

6. Removing any preinstalled crap ware

Backup is great and it can uninstall the battery draining and space wasting ware that is usually preinstalled on some phones today. The feature is root only. If you have your phone rooted, then all you have to do is to freeze them so as to allow the phone to work as it should and then delete them so as to free the space.

Rooting your Android Device

Follow these steps and you'll have a tether and other capabilities in no time. This is for anyone at any computer skill level.If you follow these instructions explicitly, and your phone is listed on the site, you will have no problems rooting your phone. Stray from the path laid out, and you may have just made yourself a $500 paper weight.

Caution: If you do not do this properly, you could brick(to turn into a worthless paperweight) your expensive to replace phone. I want to be explicitly clear: there is no warranty that this will work on your particular phone, but millions of people have successfully rooted their phones, so just follow the directions here and you'll have root access to your phone.

Step 1:
Download and unzip **unrevoked**, the easiest rooting method known to man. This works on any HTC phone, so if you have a different phone than the **Incredible 2**, just select whatever phone you have.
unrevoked.com

If you have any questions about installation or any FAQ's, go here: unrevoked wiki

Step 2:

Download and unzip the modified USB Driver for your phone available here:
http://unrevoked.com/rootwiki/doku.php/public/windows hboot driver install

Step 3:

We need to enable USB Debugging on your phone.Go to Settings>Applications>Development.Now check the check box that says USB Debugging. You now have enabled USB Debugging on your phone. Now while staying in your Development screen, plug your phone into your computer. A pop-up window should show up alerting you to a new device being plugged in, and you'll need to point your computer to the modified driver you downloaded in Step 2. Once you have the driver installed, you can now shut your phone off and unplug it from your computer.

Step 4:

While holding down the Volume Up button, hold your power button at the same time to boot your phone in to HBOOT mode. Once your phone screen looks like the picture below, plug your phone back in to your computer again and install the same USB driver again that you did in step 3.

Step 5:

Run your unrevoked.exe program that you unzipped earlier, sit back, and watch your phone being rooted. P.S. Don't touch your phone or your computer while this is happening, as this, may cause irreconcilable damage to your new paper weight.

5 essential apps after Rooting

Rooting is an illegitimate activity, and the device manufacturers don't provide support or warranty for any rooted Android device. Even after knowing all this, if you've gone ahead and rooted your Android Smartphone or tablet, then it's the time to manage and protects your device's security. Rooting Android devices might attract you to overcome limitations that hardware manufacturers put on some devices, but rooting permits a user to alter or replace system applications and other settings. Additionally, rooting your Google Android Smartphones and tablets allows you to run specialized apps that require administrator-level permissions and perform specific operations that aren't accessible to a normal Android user. If you've taken a step forward, then install these five best Android apps to ensure routine backups, access system-level files, and quickly boot into any Android mode.

1. Titanium Backup

Titanium Backup is a must installed app after rooting your device as it allows you to establish a strong security shield and protect your data files from future damages. Undoubtedly, the Android market faces plenty of uncertain threats and vulnerabilities that can damage your device to an irreparable extent so it is better to prepare yourself in advance. Android threats can easily flash your device with a kernel or a virus that might turn your device into an unresponsive phone. The app helps users by taking full backups of your device and allows them to restore the entire content later on. Users can get the app for free of cost from the Android Store and can create manual backups when they suspect any illegitimate activity or perform a custom development strategy. The app can efficiently backup your downloaded and installed apps, freeze apps, SMS, and other important files.

2. Quick Boot

This is another free app from the Google Play Store, and its key combinations allow a user to enjoy using various modes on Android devices. Using this app, you can easily access the recovery and bootloader modes or various Android modes, irrespective of your device's brand and manufacturer. The app lets you reboot into various modes with a single tap to eliminate the hassle of holding down numerous buttons on your device. The app is ideal for users who wish to access numerous UI modes and enjoy quick booting on their different Android devices.

3. ROM Manager

ROM Manager is amongst one of the best Android apps that can assist you to flash a custom recovery on a custom ROM. If you have a rooted Android gadget, then you can easily install a custom flash ROM to access the popular CWM Recovery by installing this app. Gaining access to the popular CWM Recovery will allow you to install your favorite custom firmware and reboot into the recovery mode by following a single tap technique. The app is available for free on the Google Play store, and you can download it to ensure complete device and user security.

4. AnTuTu CPU Master

Sometimes, you might feel that your Android device doesn't have the same speed and performance that impressed you during its initial purchase. AnTuTu CPU Master is an app that allows you to increase the speed of your processor and improve the overall performance to ensure smooth and faster Android experience. Additionally, you can also enjoy seamless gaming and video streaming experience, as it also boosts up your GPU and ensures faster graphics rendering. Download the app instantly for free from the official Android Store and experience tremendous improvement in your device's performance and speed!

5. Root Explorer

Root Explorer allows a user to explore the root level files on your Google Android device that you can't explore using the default file manager. The app allows you to view, modify, and even delete the unnecessary files or phone software that isn't required. But users have to be extra careful while doing so because it may lead to the bricking of your device and may cause some irreparable damages.

SQL(Structured Query Language)

SQL stands for Structured Query Language and is a declarative programming language used to access and in manipulate data RDBMS (Relational Database Management Systems). SQL was developed by IBM in 70's for their mainframe platform. Several years later SQL became standardized by both American National Standards Institute (ANSI-SQL) and International Organization for Standardization (ISO-SQL). According to ANSI SQL is pronounced "es queue el", but many software and database developers with background in MS SQL Server pronounce it "sequel".

SQL is predominantly used by 2 types of users-programs and humans (keying in the commands through a database client) to pass instructions to databases. SQL commands can be keyed into a database client like the MySQL Query Browser or the SQL Server Enterprise Manager and executed to either return a result or modify records in the database. SQL can also be used in conjunction with a programming language or scripting languages like Microsoft Visual Basic or PHP to communicate with the database.

Although SQL is a world standard, it is unfortunate that most database vendors have come up with different dialects and variations. This is because every database vendor wants to differentiate their database products from the crowd. One good example is Microsoft SQL Server's TRANSACT-SQL. TRANSACT-SQL is a superset of SQL and is designed for use only with Microsoft SQL Server. Although it does make programming much easier for software developers, it is not compliant with other databases like Oracle or MySQL making

TRANSACT-SQL programs non database-portable. As such, although many of these features are powerful and robust, it is good practice to exercise caution and limit your SQL use to be compliant with the ANSI/ISO SQL standards and ODBC-Compliant.

What is RDBMS?

A Relational Database Management System is a piece of software used to store and manage data in database objects called tables. A relational database table is a tabular data structure arranged in columns and rows. The table columns also known as table fields have unique names and different attributes defining the column type, default value, indexes and several other column characteristics. The rows of the relational database table are the actual data entries.

SQL Injection is one of the many web attack mechanisms used by hackers to steal data from organisations. It is perhaps one of the most common application layer attack techniques used today.

Web applications allow legitimate website visitors to submit and retrieve data to/from a database over the Internet using their preferred web browser.

Databases are central to modern websites they store data needed for websites to deliver specific content to visitors and render information to customers, suppliers, employees and a host of stakeholders. User credentials, financial and payment information, company statistics may all be resident within a database and accessed by legitimate users through off-the-shelf and custom web applications. Web applications and databases allow you to regularly run your business.

SQL Injection is the hacking technique which attempts to pass SQL commands through a web application for execution by the backend database. If not santised properly, web applications may result in SQL Injection attacks that allow hackers to view information from the database and/or even wipe it out.

Such features as login pages, support and product request forms, feedback forms, search pages, shopping carts and the general delivery of dynamic content, shape modern websites and provide businesses with the means necessary to communicate with prospects and customers. These website features are all examples of web applications which may be either purchased off-the-shelf or developed as bespoke programs.

These website features are all susceptible to SQL Injection attacks,

SQL Injection

Take a simple login page where a legitimate user would enter his username and password combination to enter a secure area to view his personal details or upload his comments in a forum.
When the legitimate user submits his details, an SQL query is generated from these details and submitted to the database for verification. If valid, the user is allowed access. In other words, the web application that controls the login page will communicate with the database through a series of planned commands so as to verify the

username and password combination. On verification, the legitimate user is granted appropriate access.

Through SQL Injection, the hacker may input specifically crafted SQL commands with the intent of bypassing the login form barrier and seeing what lies behind it. This is only possible if the inputs are not properly sanitised (ie., made invulnerable) and sent directly with the SQL query to the database. SQL Injection vulnerabilities provide the means for a hacker to communicate directly to the database.

The technologies vulnerable to this attack are dynamic script languages including ASP, ASP.NET, PHP, JSP, and CGI. All an attacker needs to perform an SQL Injection hacking attack is a web browser, knowledge of SQL queries and creative guess work to important table and field names. The sheer simplicity of SQL Injection has fuelled its popularity.

In SQL Injection, the hacker uses SQL queries and creativity to get to the database of sensitive corporate data through the web application.

SQL or Structured Query Language is the computer language that allows you to store, manipulate, and retrieve data stored in a relational database (or a collection of tables which organise and structure data). SQL is, in fact, the only way that a web application (and users) can interact with the database. Examples of relational databases includes Oracle, Microsoft Access, MS SQL Server, MySQL, and Filemaker Pro, all of which use SQL as their basic building blocks.

SQL commands include SELECT, INSERT, DELETE and DROP TABLE. DROP TABLE is as ominous as it sounds and in fact will eliminate the table with a particular name. In the legitimate scenario of the login page example above, the SQL commands planned for the web application may look like the following:

```
SELECT count(*)
FROM users_list_table
WHERE username='FIELD_USERNAME' AND
password='FIELD_PASSWORD
```

In plain English, this SQL command (from the web application) instructs the database to match the username and password input by the legitimate user to the combination it has already stored.

Each type of web application is hard coded with specific SQL queries that it will execute when performing its legitimate functions and communicating with the database. If any input field of the web application is not properly sanitised, a hacker may inject additional SQL commands that broaden the range of SQL commands the web application will execute, thus going beyond the original intended design and function.

A hacker will thus have a clear channel of communication (or, in layman terms, a tunnel) to the database irrespective of all the intrusion detection systems and network security equipment installed before the physical database server.

Is my database at risk to SQL Injection? SQL Injection is one of the most common application layer attacks currently being used on the Internet. Despite the fact that it is relatively easy to protect against SQL

Injection, there are a large number of web applications that remain vulnerable.

According to the Web Application Security Consortium (WASC) 9% of the total hacking incidents reported in the media until 27th July 2006 were due to SQL Injection. More recent data from our own research shows that about 50% of the websites we have scanned this year are susceptible to SQL Injection vulnerabilities.

It may be difficult to answer the question whether your web site and web applications are vulnerable to SQL Injection especially if you are not a programmer or you are not the person who has coded your web applications.
Our experience leads us to believe that there is a significant chance that your data is already at risk from SQL Injection.
Whether a attacker is able to see the data stored on the database or not, really depends on how your website is coded to display the results of the queries sent. What is certain is that the attacker will be able to execute arbitrary SQL Commands on the vulnerable system, either to compromise it or else to obtain information.
If improperly coded, then you run the risk of having your customer and company data compromised.

What an attacker gains access to also depends on the level of security set by the database. The database could be set to restrict to certain commands only. A read access normally is enabled for use by web application back ends.
Even if an attacker is not able to modify the system, he would still be able to read valuable information.

Impact of SQL Injection

Once an attacker realizes that a system is vulnerable to SQL Injection, he is able to inject SQL Query/Commands through an input form field. This is equivalent to handing the attacker your database and allowing him to execute any SQL command including DROP TABLE to the database!

An attacker may execute arbitrary SQL statements on the vulnerable system. This may compromise the integrity of your database and/or expose sensitive information. Depending on the back-end database in use, SQL injection vulnerabilities lead to varying levels of data/system access for the attacker. It may be possible to manipulate existing queries, to UNION (used to select related information from two tables) arbitrary data, use subselects, or append additional queries.

In some cases, it may be possible to read in or write out to files, or to execute shell commands on the underlying operating system.[break][break]Certain SQL Servers such as Microsoft SQL Server contain stored and extended procedures (database server functions). If an attacker can obtain access to these procedures it

Unfortunately the impact of SQL Injection is only uncoveredwhen the theft is discovered.Data is being unwittingly stolen through various hack attacks all the time. The more expert of hackers rarely get caught.

Example of a SQL Attack

The easiest way for the login.asp to work is by building a database query that looks like this:

```
SELECT id
FROM logins
WHERE username = '$username' AND password = '$password'
```

If the variables Susername and Spassword are requested directly from the user's input, this can easily be compromised. Suppose that we gave "Shashwat" as a username and that the following string was provided as a password: anything' OR 'x'='x

```
SELECT id
FROM logins
WHERE username = 'smith'
AND password = 'anything' OR 'x'='x'
```

As the inputs of the web application are not properly sanitized, the use of the single quotes has turned the WHERE SQL command into a two-component clause.

The 'x'='x' part guarantees to be true regardless of what the first part contains.

This will allow the attacker to bypass the login form without actually knowing a valid username/password combination.

How to Restore SQL Database Easily Without Any Difficulty

SQL is aapplication produced by Microsoft which is used. broadly for efficient data management by many organizations around the world and has really become an indispensable need of users all over. SQL. or the Structured Query Language helps the users to query the databases and also to easily retrieve information from databases that had been made already. In this MS SQL Server, the files are saved in .mdf file format.

With SQL. functioning normally, data management is matchlessly easy, but the real trouble arises for the users when any problem comes in this SQL Server. If you are fed up of the SQL database corruption tension which is uncalled for and also fed up of the unwanted impediment to your work because of it, then it is high time you get an SQL Server Restoring Database tool and immediately think how to restore SQL database easily without any difficulty? Only a reliable SQL restoring database software can be the ideal tension releaser that will take away the data loss fear and give way to complete satisfaction.

Why SQL gets corrupted?

Causes of SQL Server corruption are actually the reasons requiring the need for SQL recovery. The corruption is sudden and can happen unexpectedly due to several reasons like:

- ➢ Problem in hard drive
- ➢ Improper and strange system shutdown accidentally

- ➢ Virus or Trojan attack
- ➢ Software or hardware malfunction
- ➢ Incorrect String to multi-client database along with user deletion of Log file or database in "suspected" mode
- ➢ No free disk space available while the working of SQL Server
- ➢ While MS SQL. database is running, disk controllers trying to access or copy the file

These are other such abrupt and unanticipated reasons lead to SQL corruption. It is impossible to turn the time back and avoid such thing to happen. Only possibility with the user is to think How to Restore SQL if he using SQL 2005 and how to restore SQL 2000 if he is using SQL Server 2000.

Errors appearing at the time of corruption

A user can get one of the following errors at the time of SQL corruption:

- ➢ Index '%ls' on '%ls' in database '%ls' may be corrupt because of expression evaluation changes in this release.
  Drop and re-create the index
- ➢ The file *.mdf is missing and needs to restore
- ➢ Server can't find the requested database table
- ➢ Pageld in the page header = (0:0)
- ➢ Table Corrupt: Object ID 0, index ID 0, page ID (1:623)
- ➢ The process could not execute 'sp_replcmds' on server.
- ➢ Internal error. Buffer provided to read column value is too small. Run DBCC CHECKDB to check for any corruption.
- ➢ On changes table that was working.frm is locked.
- ➢ The conflict occurred in database 'db_name', table 'table name', column 'column_name'. The statement has been terminated.
- ➢ Corruption error of indexes, stored procedures, triggers and database. integrity table that should be there .MYI file is not.

Know how to restore SQL easily without any difficulty First and foremost thing which a user is required to do is to judge whether there is a need for an outside SQL restoring database tool or not. Professional help in the shape of an SQL Server recovery tool is required in case the user is getting any of the above errors because in that case recovery is only possible by using an outside software product. SysTools SQL recovery software is able to fix SQL server 2005 and 2000 database files easily without any difficulty.

SQL Web Hosting

Web Hosting is a service provided by a company that leases server space to companies or individuals that have web pages they want to display on the internet. Web hosts provide the necessary bandwidth and technology to allow internet users to access these web pages. While anyone can create a web page, special servers dedicated to internet connectivity and hosting are required to make the web page active.

Therefore, SQL web hosting is a service that allows SQL databases to be hosted on the internet. SQL web hosting can be used to store database information on the web, allow offsite personal to access database management tools and provide detailed information to customers or clients. Typical applications that use SQL databases are ERP (Enterprise Resource Planning) and CRM (Customer Relationship Management) programs.

Things to Look for in a Quality SQL Web Hosting Service

Once you've decided to go with an SQL web host, you'll need to select a service. There are a lot of providers currently on the market, and sometimes it's difficult to tell them apart. A quality SQL web hosting service should offer you the following:

- Reliability
- Control Panel Options
- Techal Support
- Customer Support
- Multiple Hosting Plans

Overall, if you plan on maintaining a database online, your best option is to go with a web hosting service that has servers dedicated specifically to SQL applications. Doing so will ensure that you get the most value out of your investment SQL web hosting may cost a little more than standard hosting, but it's worth every penny.

NETWORKING

A network is a group of computers, printers, and other devices that are connected together with cables. The sharing of data and resources. Information travels over the cables, allowing network users to exchange documents & data with each other, print to the same printers, and generally share any hardware or software that is connected to the network. Each computer, printer, or other peripheral device that is connected to the network is called a node. Networks can have tens, thousands, or even millions of nodes.

Cabling:

The two most popular types of network cabling are twisted pair (also known as 10BaseT) and thin coax (also known as 10Base2).10BaseT cabling looks like ordinary telephone wire, except that it has 8 wires inside instead of 4. Thin coax looks like the copper coaxial cabling that's often used to connect a VCR to a TV set.

Network Adapter:

A network computer is connected to the network cabling with a network interface card, (also called a "NIC", or network adapter). Some NICs are installed inside of a computer: the PC is opened up and a network card is plugged directly into one of the computer's internal expansion slots. 286, 386, and many 486 computers have 16 bit slots, so a 16-bit NIC is needed. Faster computers, like high-speed 486s and Pentiums, often have 32-bit or PCI slots. These PCs requires 32-bit NICS to achieve the fastest networking speeds possible for speed-critical applications like desktop video, multimedia, publishing, and databases. And if a computer is going to be used with a Fast Ethernet network, it will need a network adapter that supports 100Mbps data speeds as well.

Hubs

The last piece of the networking puzzle is called a hub. A hub is a box that is used to gather groups of PCs together at a central location with 10BaseT cabling. If you're networking a small group of computers together, you may be able to get by with a hub, some 10BaseT cables, and a handful of network adapters. Larger networks often use a thin coax "backbone" that connects an row of 10BaseT hubs together. Each hub, in turn, may connect a handful of computer together using 10BaseT cabling, which allows you to build networks of tens, hundreds, or thousands of nodes.

Like network cards, hubs are available in both standard (10Mbps) and Fast Ethernet (100Mbps) versions.

LANS (Local Area Networks)

A network is any collection of independent computers that communicate with one another over a shared network medium. LANs are networks usually confined to a geographic area, such as a single building or a college campus. LANS can be small, linking as few as three computers, but often link hundreds of computers used by thousands of people. The development of standard networking protocols and media has resulted in worldwide proliferation of LANS throughout business and educational organizations.

WANS (Wide Area Networks)

Often a network is located in multiple physical places. Wide area networking combines multiple LANS that that are geographically separate. This is accomplished by connecting the different LANS using services such as dedicated leased phone lines, dial-up phone lines (both synchronous and asynchronous), satellite links, and data packet carrier services. Wide area networking can be as simple as a modem and remote access server for employees to dial into, or it can be as complex as hundreds of branch offices globally linked using special routing protocols and filters to minimize the expense of sending data sent over vast distances.

Internet

The Internet is a system of linked networks that are worldwide in scope and facilitate data communication services such as remote login, file transfer, electronic mail, the World Wide Web and newsgroups. With the meteoric rise in demand for connectivity, the Internet has become a communications highway for millions of users. The Internet was initially restricted to military and academic institutions but now it is a full-fledged conduit for any and all forms of information and commerce. Internet websites now provide personal, educational, political and economic resources to every corner of the planet.

Intranet

With the advancements made in browser-based software for the Internet, many private organizations are implementing intranets. An intranet is a private network utilizing Internet type tools, but available only within that organization. For large organizations, an intranet provides an easy access mode to corporate information for employees.

Ethernet

Ethernet is the most popular physical layer LAN technology in use today. Other LAN types include Token Ring, Fast Ethernet, Fiber Distributed Data Interface (FDDI), Asynchronous Transfer Mode (ATM) and LocalTalk. Ethernet is popular because it strikes a good balance between speed, cost and ease of installation. These benefits, combined with wide acceptance in the computer marketplace and the ability to support virtually all popular network protocols, make Ethernet an ideal networking technology for most computer users today. The Institute for Electrical and Electronic Engineers (IEEE) defines the Ethernet standard as IEEE Standard 802.3.This standard defines rules for configuring an Ethernet network as well as specifying how elements in an Ethernet network interact with one another. By adhering to the IEEE standard, network equipment and network protocols can communicate efficiently.

Protocols

Network protocols are standards that allow computers to communicate. A protocol defines how computers identify one another on a network, the form that the data should take in transit, and how this information is processed once it reaches its final destination. Protocols also defines procedures for handling lost or damaged transmissions or "packets." TCP/IP (for UNIX, Windows NT, Windows 95 and other platforms), IPX (for Novell NetWare), DECnet (for networking Digital Equipment Corp. computers), AppleTalk (for Macintosh computers), and NetBIOS/NetBEUI (for LAN Manager and Windows NT networks) are the main types of network protocols in use today.

Although each network protocol is different, they all share the same physical cabling. This common method of accessing the physical network allows multiple protocols to peacefully coexist over the network media, and allows the builder of a network to use common hardware for a variety of protocols. This concept is known as "protocol independence," which means that devices that are compatible at the physical and data link layers allow the user to run many different protocols over the same medium.

Private IP address

The IP or Internet Protocol address such as 192.168.0.1 is a specific address utilized by computers for computer networks in the communication and identification process. It is the identifier for recognizing electronic devices connected to a network.

The IP address 192.168.1.1 is a personal IPv4 one. It is located between 192.168.0.0 and 192.168.255.255.You can configure any brands of network routers or computers on local networks for using it.But the address is restricted to a single device on the network for preventing address conflicts.

Private addresses are quite unusual as they can be used many times for a range of networks. It means that having the same IP address for a variety of networks at the same time doesn't cause any interferences or conflicts. And despite that, the range of private IP addresses is considered to be non-routable which means these addresses are not able to communicate on the Internet as routers are set to block the entry traffic delivered via private addresses. This may be their disadvantage but it might be an advantage in another way. As outer networks do not connect to private ones, this IP address will not be vulnerable to the nasty elements such as irresponsible or bad users.

If there is a necessity to link to outer networks, this private address has to do a gateway, so that other networks can detect it. A router may also allow the Internet use between these both networks. In order to have this happen, you need a proxy server or NAT (Network Address Translation). In any event note that two networks might have the same IP address. Also some arousal problems in accessing the router are possible. Browser settings need to be cleared for that.

The Internet Protocol (IP) address is a exclusive address used by computers for a computer network in the identification and communication processes. It is used as an identifier to recognize electronic devices connected on a network. Hence each device is subjected to a unique address.

WIRELESS LANS WLAN

COMPARING WLAN to a LAN

The dominant IEEE 802 groups are 802.3 & 802.11

However, there are important differences between the two

Radio Frequency has no boundaries like a wire so data frames travel to anyone that can receive Radio Frequency signals. Radio Frequency is un protected from outside signals.

Radio Frequency has some unique challenges, The further from the source the weaker the transmission.

Radio Frequency bands are regulated differently in different countries. In a wireless topology, a wireless AP can be used instead of a switch.

WLANS hosts contend for access to the Radio Frequency media.

802.11 uses collision avoidance instead of Collision detection.

WLANS use a different frame format than ethernet LANs.

WLANS require additional info in the L2.

WLANS raise privacy issues since RF can reach outside the facility.

INTRO TO WIRELESS LANS

802.11 LANS extend the 802.3 infrastructure to provide additional connectivity options.

Requires additional components & protocols

In 802.3 the switch is the AP for clients

In 802.11 clients use a wireless adapter to access a wireless router or AP.

Once connected wireless clients can access resources just as if they were wired.

WLAN STANDARDS

802.11 uses the unlicensed industrial, scientific, medical (ISM) frequencies for the physical & mac sub layer.

Early 802.11 was 2 MBS @ 2.4 GHz

Standards improved with 11a, 11b, 11g, 11n
802.11a &g=54MBs
802.11b 11MBs
802.11n appear to have a rate greater than 100Mbs

OFDM is faster & more expensive to implement than DSSS

802.11a

OFDM 5GHz, less prone to interference, smaller antennas

Poor range & performance susceptible to obstructions

802.11b & g both use 2.4 GHz

802.11b uses DSSS

802.11g uses OFDM & DSSS

2.4GHz has better range & not as easily obstructed, but still prone to interference

802.11n

Improves data & range without new RF band Uses multiple input multi output (IMMO) technology Theoretical 248Mbs

Expected to be ratified by sept 08

RF bands allocated by ITU-R

Bands administered by the FCC,CRTC

Wi-Fi Certification

WiFi cert is provided by the WiFi

Standards ensure interoperability

Three key organizations influencing WLAN standards are

ITU-R:allocates RF bands

IEEE: specifies how RF is modulated WIFI Alliance: interportability across vendors The WiFi alliance certifies all 3 IEEE 802.11 standards as well as IEEE drafts & the WPA WPA2 standards based on 802.11i. WIRELESS NICS

Uses the config modulation tech encoded a data stream onto an RF signal

Early wireless NICS were cards PCMCIA but are built into laptops now

PCI & USB Nics are available as well

WIRELESS ACCESS POINTS

Clients do not typically communicate directly to each

AN AP connects clients to wired LAN and converts tcp-ip packets from 802.11 to 802.3 frames.

Clients must associate with an AP to obtain net services. An AP is an L2 device that functions like an Ethernet hub.Radio Frequency is a shared medium just like early Ethernet buses. Devices that want to use the medium must contend for it. Wireless NIC's cannot detect collisions, so instead they must avoid them.

Importance Of Wireless Encryption

Wireless networks are everywhere. You'll find them in airports, trains, cafe's, businesses, homes, and many other places. Consumers commonly work with sensitive data on the internet such as financial records, medical records, and sensitive emails. Since wireless networks have become so common, it's important to understand why you should encrypt your connection as well as the risks that surface when you choose to leave your wireless network unsecured. In the realm of networking, there are many vectors for attack on open wireless networks. It is substantially easier for someone to gain unauthorized access to your computer and files if they are on your network with you. In addition, it is possible that the attacker will analyze the traffic on your network, allowing him to see what sites you visit and to potentially steal your credentials for various sites. Other risks you face are less serious, but still aggravating and difficult to mitigate. The attacker on your network may choose not to gain access to your computer or analyze your traffic, but instead perform a denial of service attack. This type of attack floods the network (or just your computer if that's the case) with requests, making it incredibly difficult and in most cases impossible to access the internet and network.

Setting up your wireless network to incorporate encryption isn't hard, and in most cases will only take a few minutes. Every wireless router has a different method to change the settings for your network, and once you know how to access those settings, it's a matter of a few clicks and typing in a password. WEP encryption should never be used to encrypt a wireless network. The encryption can be cracked very easily with the right tools and usually in less than 3 minutes.WPA and WPA2 are currently the best choices for wireless encryption; WPA2 being the better option of the two.

Host Scanning

What is port scanning you might ask? Well, port scanning can be describe many ways, but basically is the act of sending packets to a destination of group of hosts to try to get a response. Why do I need to port scan and do others port scan me? You might want to port scan your broadband connection to see what your network has open to the internet and others may port scan you to find a way into your network. Port scanning can be done for good reasons and malicious purposes. Other real good reasons for port scanning is to see what ports your software might be using this can help you trouble shoot network issues. There are too many reasons to list here on the pros of ports scans and port scan software but you must first understand what a port is and how it affects your computer and network.

What is a port and how dose it work?

Ports are similar to addresses for example if you send a package to a friend you will have to put many entries on the shipping label for it to get to him. You would need a name, street number, city, State, zip code, and sometimes a country.Without this information your package would not get the recipient. Ports work in a similar way. Ports are part of the address for internet traffic. Ports also have to have other data to be used like an IP address, Protocol, and transport media.

Who controls port numbers?

Ports numbers are standardized though the "Internet Assigned Numbers Authority" or IANA. The port numbers are divided into three ranges: The Well Known Ports, Registered Ports, and the Dynamic and/or Private Ports. The Well Known Ports are those from 0 through 1023. DCCP

Well Known ports SHOULD NOT be used without IANA registration. The registration procedure is defined in [RFC4340], Section 19.9.

The Registered Ports are those from 1024 through 49151 DCCP Registered ports SHOULD NOT be used without IANA registration. The registration procedure is defined in [RFC4340], Section 19.9.

The Dynamic and/or Private Ports are those from 49152 through 65535.

Port Scanning Software

Let's now take a look at software that is used for port scanning. An lot of the software out there for port scanning also has other futures for vulnerability scanning. One of the most well known port scanning tools is NMAP.

Nmap ("Network Mapper") is a free open source utility for network exploration or security auditing. It was designed to rapidly scan large networks, although it works fine against single hosts. Nmap uses raw IP packets in novel ways to determine what hosts are available on the network, what services (application name and version) those hosts are offering, what operating systems (and OS versions) they are running, what type of packet filters/firewalls are in use, and dozens of other characteristics. Nmap runs on most types of computers and both console and graphical versions are available. Nmap is free and open source (description from NMAP's website).

Angry IP scanner is a very fast IP scanner and port scanner. It can scan IP addresses in any range as well as any their ports. Its binary file size is very small compared to other IP or port scanners. Angry IP scanner simply pings each IP address to check if it's alive, then optionally it is resolving its hostname, determines the MAC address, scans ports, etc. The amount of gathered data about each host can be extended with the available plugin's (description from angryziber.com).

SuperScan 4 is a Powerful TCP port scanner, pinger, and resolver. Here are some of the futures; Superior scanning speed, Support for unlimited IP ranges, Improved host detection using multiple ICMP methods, TCP SYN scanning, UDP scanning (two methods), IP address import supporting ranges and CIDR formats, Simple HTML report generation, Source port scanning, Fast hostname resolving, Extensive banner grabbing, Massive built-in port list description database, IP and port scan order randomization, A selection of useful tools (ping, trace route, Whois, etc). SuperScan is from foundstone.com and this description was gathered from there website.

Online Scanners

There are also websites that offer free port scans to help you secure your network. Here is a list of a few scanning sites.
Sygate Online Scan (scan.sygate.com) extended security check (Stealth Scan, Trojan Scan.

Planet Security Firewall-Check (planet-security.net) Fast, extended check, checks currently high-endangered ports.

Crucialtests (crucialtests.com) concise, incl. advisor.

ShieldsUP (grc.com) Quick Scanner, clearly laid out.

How to block all the scanning

Now that you have seen what ports scanning is and the uses for it you might want to know how to protect you network from scans. The best thing to do is have a firewall and use up-to-date Anti-virus & Anti-Spyware programs. You will not be able to stop the scans on your network but with a good firewall the person scanning you will not see any traffic back and hopefully assume your connection is not on or no assemble.

How A Port Scan Works

With many new security threats arriving everyday, protecting your computer and digital files is even more important. One threat today is port scanning. Port scanning happens to most people whether they realize it or not. Protecting yourself against port scans can help you secure your system from malicious users.

All computers have ports, and services run on these ports. When your computer needs to connect to your mail server in order to check your email, it will open one of these ports and make a connection to download your new email. However sometimes these ports are always on and listening. A port scan occurs when attacker scans a host to see which ports are open and which are closed or not in use.

Think of a port scan like checking doors and windows of your house to see if it is locked or not. While, the attacker may not break into your house he may know that there is a window unlocked and entry can be achieved easily. A port scanner works in much the same way as it checks ports on your computer to see which is closed or open. It is not illegal in most places to do a port scan because your just checking if the connection can be made and not actually making a connection to the host. However it is possible to create a Denial of Service attack if port scans are made repeatedly.

Many firewalls can protect you against port scans. A firewall is a program that monitors outgoing and incoming connections to your computer. A firewall may open all ports on your system to effectively stop scans from showing any ports. While this approach works in many cases.Port Scans have advanced with new techniques such as ICMP port unreachable scans and NULL scans. While its best to try and filter all port scans to your computer, its also important to realize that any ports that are open and listening need to be investigated Leaving open ports on your machine can lead to a system compromise causing lost data, and possibly identity theft. A port scan of your own system can show you exactly what an attacker sees and what sort of action you need to take to prevent an attack on your system.

One of the most popular port scanners available today is NMap from insecure.org. NMap is available for free download and is available for UNIX and Windows based systems. Its important to understand how NMap works so you can take the same approach as an attacker would against you. There are other port scanning software available and each has their own port scanning features. However, NMap is by far the most popular and is loaded with features, and different sorts of port scans you can perform.

Detecting Network Sniffers

A packet sniffer is a program or device that eavesdrops on network traffic and gathers data from packets. Sometimes such wiretaps are carried out by the network administrator for beneficial purposes (like intrusion detection, performance analysis, etc.). On the other hand, malicious intruders may install packet sniffers in order to retrieve clear-text usernames and passwords from the local network or other vital information transmitted on the network. Vulnerable protocols (with clear-text passwords) include telnet, pop3, imap, ftp, smtp-auth and NNTP. Sniffers work because ethernet was designed to be shared. Most networks use broadcast technology-- messages for one computer can be read by another computer on that network. In practice, computers ignore messages except those that were sent directly to them (or broadcast to all hosts on the network). However, computers can be placed in promiscuous mode and made to accept messages even if they are not meant for them-- this is how a Sniffer works.
People assume that computers connected to a switch a safe from sniffing - - but this is not so. Computers connected to switches are just as vulnerable to sniffers as those connected to a hub. are

How a Sniffer works

A computer connected to a LAN has 2 addresses -- one is the MAC address that uniquely identifies each node in a network and which is stored on the network card. The MAC address is used by the ethernet protocol when building frames to transfer data. The other is the IP address, which is used by applications. The Data Link Layer (layer 2 of the OSI model) uses an ethernet header with the MAC address of the destination machine. The Network Layer (layer 3 of the OS model) is responsible for mapping IP network addresses to the MAC address as required by the Data Link Protocol Layer 3 attempts to look-up the MAC address of the destination machine in a table, called the ARP cache. If no MAC entry is found for the IP address, the Address Resolution Protocol broadcasts a request packet (ARP request) to all machines on the network. The machine with that IP address responds to the source machine with its MAC address. This MAC address then gets added to the source machines ARP Cache. This MAC address is then used by the source machine in all its communications with the destination machine.

There are two basic types of ethernet environments shared and switched. In a shared ethernet environment all hosts are connected to the same bus and compete with one another for bandwidth. In such an environment packets meant for one machine are received by all the other machines. All the computers on the shared ethernet compare the frame's destination MAC address with their own. If the two don't match, the frame is quietly discarded. A machine running a sniffer breaks this rule and accepts all frames. Such a machine is said to have been put into promiscuous mode and can effectively listen to all the traffic on the network. Sniffing in a shared ethernet environment is passive and, hence, difficult to detect.

In a switched environment, the hosts are connected to a switch instead of a hub. The switch maintains a table that keeps track of each computer's MAC address and the physical port on the switch to which that MAC address is connected. The switch is an intelligent device which sends packets only to the destination computer. As a result, the process of putting a machine into promiscuous mode to gather packets does not work. However, this does not mean that switched networks are secure and cannot be sniffed.

Though a switch is more secure than a hub, you can use the following methods to sniff on a switch:

• ARP Spoofing - - The ARP is stateless, that is, you can send an ARP reply even if none has not been asked for, and such a reply will be accepted. For example, one technique is to ARP Spoof the gateway of the network. The ARP cache of the targeted host will now have a wrong entry for the gateway and is said to be Poisoned. From this point on, all the traffic destined for the gateway will pass through the sniffer machine. Another trick that can be used is to poison a host's ARP cache by setting the gateway's MAC address to FF:FF:FF:FF:FF:FF (also known as the broadcast MAC).

• MAC Flooding - - Switches keep a translation table that maps MAC addresses to physical ports on the switch. This allows them to intelligently route packets from one host to another. The switch has a limited amount of memory for this work, MAC flooding makes use of this limitation to bombard a switch with fake MAC addresses until the switch can't keep up. The switch then enters into what is known as a 'failopen mode', at which point it starts acting as a hub by broadcasting packets to all the machines on the network. Once that happens sniffing can be performed easily.

Detecting Sniffers on the Network

A sniffer is usually passive -- it just collects data -- and is especially difficult to detect when running in a shared Ethernet environment. However, it is easy to detect a sniffer when installed on a switched network. When installed on a computer a sniffer does generate some small amount of traffic which allows for its detection using the following types of techniques:

• Ping Method -- a ping request is sent with the IP address of the suspect machine but not its MAC address. Ideally, nobody should see this packet as each ethernet adapter will reject it as it does not match its MAC address. But if the suspect machine is running a sniffer it will respond since it accepts all packets.

• ARP Method -- this method relies on the fact all machines cache ARPS (i.e. MAC addresses). Here, we send a non broadcast ARP so only machines in promiscuous mode will cache our ARP address. Next, we send a broadcast ping packet with our IP, but a different MAC address. Only a machine which has our correct MAC address from the sniffed ARP frame will be able to respond to our broadcast ping request.

On Local Host if a machine has been compromised a hacker may have left a sniffer running. There are utility programs that can be run which report whether the local machine's network adapter has been set to promiscuous mode.

• Latency Method -- is based on the assumption most sniffers do some kind of parsing, thereby increasing the load on that machine. Therefore it will take additional time to respond to a ping packet. This difference in response times can be used as an indicator of whether a machine is in promiscuous mode or not.

• ARP Watch to prevent a hacker from ARP spoofing the gateway there are utilities that can be used to monitor the ARP cache of a machine to see if there is duplication for a machine.

How To Protect Against Sniffing

The best way to secure a network against sniffing is to use encryption. While this won't prevent sniffers from functioning, it will ensure the data collected by sniffers is un interpretable. Also, on a switched network, the chances are ARP spoofing will be used for sniffing purposes. The machine that the hacker will most likely ARP-spoof is the default gateway. To prevent this from happening it is suggested the MAC address of the gateway be permanently added to each host's ARP cache.

• Use SSH instead of telnet.

• Use HTTPS instead of HTTP (if the site supports it).

• If concerned about email privacy, try a service such as Hushmail (www.hushmail.com), which uses SSL to ensure that data is not read in transit. Also, Pretty Good Privacy (www.gnupg.org) can be used for encrypting and signing emails to prevent others from reading them.

• Employ a sniffer detector. For example, the software package **PromiScan** is considered the standard sniffing node detection tool and is recommended by the SANS (SysAdmin, Audit, Network, Security) Institute. It is an application package used to remotely monitor computers on local networks to locate network interfaces operating in a promiscuous mode.

How to Dodge ARP Poisoning

A Successful ARP poisoning is invisible to the user. Since the end user is unaware of ARP poisoning he will browse the internet normally while the attacker is collecting data from the session. The data collected may be passwords, banking accounts, emails and websites. This is known as "Man in the Middle Attack."

How does this happen? The attacker sends poisoned ARP request to the gateway router device. The gateway router is now brainwashed, to think that the route to any PC through the Subnet needs to pass through the attackers PC. On the other hand, all hosts on the subnet think that the attacker PC/MAC is the actual gateway and they send all traffic and information to this computer. However, the attacker PC forwards all this data to the gateway.

Therefore there is one attacker PC that sees all traffic on the network. And if this attack is aimed at one single PC the attacker can just Spoof this victims PC to his own and only effect on the network. The attackers PC has to be really fast as the gateway has large routing tables and many sessions are running in parallel. Most regular PCs cannot handle a large inflow of data and this causes the network to freeze or crash. This happens as the attackers PC is not compatible enough and the number packets have dropped as the PC is unable to keep up with the flow of large volumes of data.

Most people are prejudiced to think that using a PC from the safe corner of their home is the best option. Here is some news for them, until and unless you do not have a firewall installed on the internet connection, there is always a danger of spoofing of outbound data from your home PC. If you are using wireless, it is important to encrypt it, otherwise you would be drawing undue attention from attackers. In order to prevent a hacker form spoofing the gateway there are various utilities that can be employed to monitor the ARP Cache of a machine to see if, there is any duplication for a machine.

However, the best way to secure a network against sniffing is encryption. Now, you may not be able to stop attackers from sniffing, but the data that they receive would be made un interpretable. Also, on a switched network, the chances are ARP spoofing would be used for sniffing purposes.

Kali Linux

Kali Linux is a Debian-based Linux distribution aimed at advanced Penetration Testing and Security Auditing. Kali contains several hundred tools which are geared towards various information security tasks, such as Penetration Testing, Security research, Computer Forensics and Reverse Engineering. Kali Linux is developed, funded and maintained by Offensive Security, a leading information security training company.

Kali Linux is specifically tailored to the needs of penetration testing professionals, and therefore all documentation on this site assumes prior knowledge of, and familiarity with, the Linux operating system in general.

Some Useful links For You

https://evilzone.org
https://hackforums.net
https://www.hackthisissite.org/forums
https://www.owasp.org
https://www.exploit-db.com
https://www.crackingforum.com
https://pastebin.com
https://www.offensive-security.com
https://offensivecommunity.net

Dark Web

1. Darkode
2. Hell
3. HackBB
4. MazaF-ka
5. TCF

I tried my best to make this book as useful as it can to you all and to be under Guidelines Issued by Our Govt. In this book, I only tried to give you a brief idea or an overview of the topic of Hacking and also tried to break down some Myths about hacking as you all know all the authors of these types of books have to work under some limits issued by our Govts. So none of us can't provide 100% knowledge to you through any platform many of you may also have searched for Hacking related things on YouTube and other platforms but were unable to find any sort of videos or unclear videos so; I will suggest you all go through this book once and then try or experiment something from that.

At last, as this is my first book so I need support from all the readers and will be waiting for your feedback on Instagram **@shas_hwat001** if you want books on some specific topic like Kali Linux, Networking, SQL, etc. I'll be eagerly waiting for your suggestions.

I'll also recommend you to watch these movies if you are interested and get time to watch:

1. Hacker(2016)
2. Snowden(2016)
3. Blackhat(2015)
4. Algorithm(2014)
5. The Social Network(2010)
6. Die Hard 4(2007)
7. Firewall(2006)
8. Hackers(1995)